LIS
→ WEST MOB
(W3M) 2/23

WITHDRAWN

CORNWALL COUNCIL

24 HOUR RENEWAL HOTLINE 0845 607 6119
www.cornwall.gov.uk/Library

THE FINAL WHISTLE

Nigel Owens

with Paul Abbandonato

First impression: 2022

© Copyright Nigel Owens and Y Lolfa Cyf., 2022

The contents of this book are subject to copyright, and may
not be reproduced by any means, mechanical or electronic,
without the prior, written consent of the publishers.

The publishers wish to acknowledge the support of
Cyngor Llyfrau Cymru

Cover photograph: Inpho photography, IRFU
Cover design: Sion Ilar

ISBN: 978 1 912631 31 5

Published and printed in Wales
on paper from well-maintained forests by
Y Lolfa Cyf., Talybont, Ceredigion SY24 5HE
website www.ylolfa.com
e-mail ylolfa@ylolfa.com
tel 01970 832 304
fax 832 782

Contents

Foreword
by Dan Carter

THERE IS, AND will only ever be, one Nigel Owens. He is a truly unique sporting figure, a rugby referee who charmed the players, was loved by supporters right throughout the world and whose off-the-field story provides inspiration to so many.

You get a few people in rugby, and sport in general, who tend to stand out because of their characteristics, but who also have real expertise in their field and are right at the top of their game. Nigel has always been one of those, an incredible character whose sheer love of rugby union always came across loud and clear.

When those individuals leave the game, they are invariably missed. Nigel will be, now that he has retired from the international arena. I just feel honoured and fortunate to have been playing my rugby for New Zealand in the same era that Nigel was refereeing. To be involved in high-profile matches refereed by a man of his calibre and level of excellence was always a privilege.

Heck, he even told me off once for swearing during the 2015 World Cup final when we played Australia at Twickenham. We were chatting away during a break in play and Nigel, aware of the microphone on his jersey, suddenly said with a smile, 'Shhh, don't swear now, you're on telly mun.' He was right, too, as he normally is.

They made some T-shirts of that comment, but they could have done that with so many of Nigel's famous sayings which enchanted the rugby public, including the 'This is Not Soccer' remark he'd occasionally say whilst trying to tell a player not to show dissent.

I think what happened between us that afternoon on the Twickenham turf perfectly embodies what makes Nigel so special. Just think of the pressures of the World Cup final, all that scrutiny upon him with millions across the globe watching his every decision. The biggest game of his career, knowing it was the biggest match of the players' careers, yet he could still make a light-hearted comment like that one to me. It showed one of the beauties of Nigel, that he was always able to enjoy himself out on the field, despite the intensity that goes with rugby at that very highest of levels.

It's part of this incredible balance Nigel was able to strike. He was clearly knowledgeable, a master of his craft, the number one referee in the world for so many years. Yet, whilst he was being assertive towards us, the players also couldn't help but like, listen to and respect him. And, indeed, smile with him. His communication skills were outstanding. To be able to have banter with the players, laugh and joke, is amazing really when you think about it. Nigel could certainly never be accused of being a robot referee.

Personally, I could never deal with the pressures of being a referee but, as I say, I feel lucky to have been playing my rugby during an era where Nigel was number one in the world and took charge of a lot of our games with the All

Blacks. He had a confidence about him, a good feel for the game, knew what to penalise players for and what to let go. He possessed these traits in abundance, but what really stood out for me was his sheer love of the game and how that would come across so clearly in his refereeing.

He was often smiling, joking and chatting with the players throughout the 80 minutes. There was a bond between referee and players, a kind of camaraderie, but we were never ever left in any doubt as to who was in charge. Nigel would listen and show empathy, but his word was always final.

He really did leave his impact on rugby union. As players, we know we were refereed by one of the best to ever do the job.

I thank Nigel for everything he has done for our great sport, the help he's given to so many outside of rugby, and the character and professionalism he has always shown. I wish him the very best for the future as he settles into his new career as a farmer back in his native Wales, though I suspect he'll be popping up on our TV screens every now and again to talk about refereeing controversies from particular matches.

Because it's Nigel, we'll listen, take note and learn.

As I say, Nigel Owens is one of a kind.

DAN CARTER
(1,598 Test points in 112 All Blacks games
between 2003–2015, World Cup winner)

Acknowledgements

IN MEMORY OF my mum Mair, 1946–2009, and with thanks to my dad Geraint.

The love, care, support and guidance you gave from day one, teaching me the values of respect, have made me who I am today.

I miss mum every single day. I wish she could have seen my major refereeing achievements over the past decade or so, but I know she'd have been incredibly proud of what I went on to accomplish after some dark times, during which she offered greater support than anybody. I would give anything to spend another minute with her.

When mum passed away, dad was still there following my career closely, immensely proud himself and helping in everything I do. After each match he is the first person I'd speak to about my performance, even ahead of my coach or referees' manager. Dad has always been very honest in his views and I greatly respect everything he has to say.

To Barrie, my partner, a big thank you for all your love and support, and I must say patience too on occasions! I don't know how I would manage without you.

I'd like to say a huge thank you also to everyone in my home village of Mynyddcerrig and the surrounding area for the support they have given me through bad times, as well as good. I know when I refereed the World Cup final it was a big thing for them. It was like a carnival in the village for a week, bunting was put up. It meant a lot to them that one of their own was chosen for rugby's biggest match, but it meant just as much to me that it meant a lot to them. *Diolch*.

To all my family and friends for being there for me, in the good times, and the tough ones too. Your continuing support means so much and I am forever grateful.

To the Welsh Rugby Union, I can't thank you enough for being such wonderful employers, so very supportive from the day I first became a professional referee. The backing through difficult times will never be forgotten. The huge role played by the WRU in helping to make rugby more diverse should be appreciated by all.

World Rugby have also been fabulous to me, as have fellow referees, players, coaches and supporters everywhere. I can't thank everybody individually – I'd need five chapters on their own to do that – but they know who they are.

To Lefi Gruffudd and Y Lolfa, thank you for coming to me in 2005 and asking me to do my first book *Hanner Amser/Half Time*, when I was a nobody really. Not that I'm anything special today, let me stress, but I'm grateful for the opportunity to tell the story of my subsequent rise to the very top of rugby refereeing, and to Paul Abbandonato for helping to ensure my words about it all make sense. A massive thank you to New Zealand all-time great Dan Carter for writing the Foreword to *The Final Whistle*. When I read what he had to say about me, it brought a tear to my eye. It means so much from a player of that stature.

Lastly, but most certainly not least, I want to say thank

you to Joe Public, not just here in my native Wales, but also throughout the UK and indeed the world. I am so grateful for the warmth, affection and goodwill you have shown me over the years. On the occasions I've received horrible abuse on social media, the messages of support and love from ordinary, decent people helped me carry on when there might have been occasions when I even thought of packing it all in.

I haven't met most of Joe Public, of course, but I'm eternally grateful.

Love to all.

Prologue

Twickenham, October 2015 – World Cup Final

I'm feeling on top of the world. I really am. Absolutely buzzing.

I've just refereed what many believe to be the greatest World Cup final of them all, New Zealand versus Australia at Twickenham, two teams full of brilliant players producing a wonderful showpiece. Prince Harry, who loves his rugby and would always make a point of shouting, 'Have a good one, Nige', every time he saw me at a game, has just presented me with my medal, or a golden whistle, to be more precise. Crikey, some of the 80,000 crowd inside this iconic sporting venue even cheered when my name was called to walk up onto the rostrum.

'Nigel, you should be so proud. I've never heard anything like this before,' the head of World Rugby's referees, the hugely respected Frenchman Joël Jutge, told me as he listened to what was happening.

It can hardly get any better than this. The way rugby union has rallied around and supported me since I announced I was gay, and indeed once tried to take my life because I didn't want to be gay, has been truly humbling and indeed amazing.

So much has happened to me since I opened up on those dark times in my first book, *Hanner Amser/Half Time*, which was published back in 2008. The World Cup final was the pinnacle, but I also went on to referee a record 100 Test matches and, unbeknown to me at the time, and most certainly unintended, videos clips of some of my so-called famous and funny sayings to players even started to go viral on social media.

'This is Not Soccer', words I first uttered to an Italian player because of the dissent he was displaying towards me, is the phrase many appear to associate with me, I guess. I wasn't trying to be clever, funny, or get shares on Facebook and Twitter. This was me as a referee just trying to exert some authority and stamp out something which we all know blights football when you see players surrounding a referee.

I'm told there were lots of other sayings which started to follow suit in terms of social media likes and popularity. Not that I took much notice. I guess because of my back story, the high-profile matches I was covering and the World Cup final itself, people were beginning to latch on to a lot of things Nigel Owens started to say or do.

Everything just sort of started to explode for me. Thus, given what has happened in those ensuing years, with the reach now being much greater than it was back in 2008 because of what I went on to achieve, I do need to tell the story of my troubled times again, albeit in a different way. If anything, it is perhaps even more appropriate all these years on as it has proved that an openly gay person can thrive in the macho world of a sport like rugby and reach the very top of their profession.

The World Cup final is evidence of that, so are those 100 Tests, the record number of Six Nations matches for a referee, plus seven European Cup club finals.

The lift-off for all of that happening, and indeed much,

much more on top, began when I stopped living a lie and accepted who I am, something that should apply to anybody in any walk of life, whatever his or her career. If my story helps other people out there who are struggling to cope with their own inner demons, then some good has come from it.

I didn't know how rugby would react, whether players, coaches, officials, fellow referees and supporters would accept me for who I really am.

Rugby reacted absolutely brilliantly. My record at the very highest level, and the support I have received from everywhere, tells me that.

Why did I even doubt it?

April 1996 – the darkest hour

Nineteen years earlier I was at rock bottom. Sitting on top of a mountain near my home, armed with a bottle of pills and a shotgun, ready to take my own life. I couldn't carry on like this any more, I needed to end it the only way I thought how.

I knew I was gay. I didn't want to be gay. I'd been to my doctor to ask to be cured. I'd read in a newspaper column you could be chemically castrated. He gently explained, 'Nigel, it doesn't work like that. But I can put you in touch with someone to talk to about it.'

I didn't want to talk to anybody. It was hard enough even plucking up the courage to tell my doctor. I left the surgery that day in an even lower mood, the suicidal thoughts increased.

I was lucky the night when I tried to end it that the pills did their job and I slipped into a deep coma. If they hadn't, I've no doubts I would have used the shotgun.

None of those refereeing records I went on to achieve would have been possible without my terrified mum alerting the authorities, the search party who found me on that damp, miserable morning and the wonderful medics at the hospital who saved me. I can never thank them enough. I really can't.

When I first told this story in *Hanner Amser*, the book was launched at my local rugby club in the west Wales village of Pontyberem, and I started receiving threatening and homophobic phone calls at the house, at all hours. Anonymous, of course, but forcibly along the lines of, call off the book launch or I'd regret it. There were even some posters put up in prominent places around the village with obscene and homophobic language used about me.

This all worried me, made me think twice about the launch. What if they turned up on the night with obscene banners and made a show of things. My mum was very sick at the time, she'd been diagnosed with terminal cancer. I didn't want her and dad having to see and hear this sort of rubbish being said about their son.

Enough was enough. I reported it to the police. My good friend Melonie Jenkins, who was the store manager at the local CK supermarket, said she had an idea who it might be as she'd seen someone parked near to where one of the posters had been placed. The police looked into the matter, identified an elderly man living in the nearby village of Bancffosfelen as the culprit, and he was dealt with and given a warning. His wife was from the same village as I was born, so naturally this upset me further.

I was shaken up, left in two minds about what to do, but realised he was the one in the wrong. There are some horrible people out there, and there was no need to waste my time thinking about it. We were going ahead with the launch as planned.

I'm so pleased that we did. Some leading Welsh rugby figures, Wales' all-time leading try-scorer Shane Williams among them, turned up. So too did top TV figures and actors, the club that night was absolutely packed to the rafters.

Most importantly, though, my mum was there. It proved to be the last time she left the house before passing away. She was incredibly proud so many people had taken the time and trouble to turn up for her son like this.

I miss her every single day. She was the one who saved my life. In the hospital, during those dark days, she told me, 'If you ever do anything like that again you may as well take me and your dad with you. We don't want to live our lives without you in it.'

We held hands and cried. I realised at that moment this is who I am, there is no choice. The pressure of doing the World Cup final was nothing compared to accepting that.

My life had been saved.

Today, the farm and the future

My 17-year career as an international referee came to an end with my 100th Test match. France versus Italy in Paris. A comfortable home win, as you might expect for one of the strong favourites for the 2023 World Cup.

Yet, far from having withdrawal symptoms at hanging up the whistle, I'm really enjoying and looking forward to my new life as a farmer with my partner Barrie, who is a primary school teacher. We live together in Pontyberem, around 17 miles north-west of Swansea and near to where I was brought up. We would love to have a couple of children; indeed we're going through the adoption process.

From a young age farming, rather than refereeing, was my dream and whilst officiating in matches throughout the world I always kept an eye out for any smallholding that might be for sale back home. It started with a few fields around the house, but grew really quickly. I now own nearly 90 acres of land and look after 75 pedigree Herefords. Yes, I do the work myself and it's full-on – mucking out, mowing the hay, moving the cattle from one field to another, normal farmer's work – but I love it, I really do.

Think refereeing the World Cup final in front of watching millions across the globe is stressful? Try delivering a calf in the middle of the night with no-one around, knowing if it's coming out backwards you'll have to pull it, or else it will die. Again, that's real pressure. Trust me, that tests your resolve in every sense. Thankfully, although he's never seen me stressed with rugby, whatever the magnitude of the match, Barrie remains calm at times like this, sees things for what they really are and helps put me at ease.

Officially, I hung up my whistle as a professional referee when my contract ran out in the summer of 2022, although I now have a new deal with my Welsh Rugby Union employers to help coach and guide younger officials coming through the system. So I'm assisting others today, just as so many offered me help and support when I first took up the whistle. It's great to put something back into a sport that has been so supportive of me.

I'm also really excited to have landed a new role as a selector on the Match Officials' Panel in the United Rugby Championship, again hoping to use my own experience to help groom referees in our league to become among the very best in the world.

It all means life continues to be really busy and rewarding. It's been some journey to get to this point, mind, particularly the last 11 years or so when I was fortunate enough to be regarded as the number one referee in the world for a long period, enjoyed being in the middle for some of rugby's greatest matches, interacting with world-class players, dealing with brilliant, sometimes headstrong coaches, even having countless conversations – and the odd row – with supporters on social media.

Memories on and off the field have been created which are very special, ones I will never forget. The dark days just turned into bright sunshine.

I share these moments with you in this book. I hope you enjoy coming on the journey with me.

CHAPTER ONE

Breaking
down barriers

THE LETTER WAS simply addressed, 'Nigel Owens, referee, Welsh Rugby Union.'

As I opened the envelope and started to scan the handwritten note, tears welled up in my eyes. I couldn't stop them. Still struggle today when I write these words, if I'm honest. It was from a mum who lived in a small village just outside Exeter.

'Dear Nigel,' she began. 'I'd like to thank you for saving my son's life …'

She went on to explain that he'd tried to commit suicide at the age of 16 because he was struggling to come to terms with being gay. They managed to find him in time, but were terrified he would try to do it again. Just like me, he wouldn't tell his parents why.

The letter struck a chord with me as it brought back memories of how, several years earlier, I too was scared witless to tell my own mum and dad about my sexuality and attempted to take my own life. How could I do that to them? The very people I loved the most.

Eventually, realising the error of my ways, I came out. It

was the best thing I have done. Ever. Suddenly, having lived a lie for so many years, I could be myself.

Naturally I worried at first how the macho world of rugby union would react to one of its leading referees being gay. This, of course, was unchartered territory at the time. There was no-one who'd come out in the professional game so I couldn't judge how the land lay. There was no-one for me to look up to, no role models to get some inspiration or courage from.

My fears, of course, proved totally and utterly unfounded. The support I received, from players, coaches, fans, those in authority and fellow referees, was overwhelming.

I went on to referee the World Cup final, officiated at four World Cups in total, took charge of more Six Nations games than anyone else and, indeed, a record-breaking 100 Test matches. Some of those were viewed by pundits, players and fans alike as among the greatest matches in rugby history. Like New Zealand's 38–27 win over South Africa in Johannesburg in 2013, an absorbing 80 minutes full of breathtaking tries, thrilling fast-paced rugby, huge tackles, and which was dubbed the 'Match of the Century'. Having been right in the thick of it, who was I to argue?

There were other matches that have gone into rugby folklore. The best World Cup final of the lot, in the view of many, as the All Blacks edged past Australia in front of a spellbound Twickenham crowd in the autumn of 2015. Eddie Jones' England beating Australia 44–40 in a 2016 Sydney rip-roarer. England again, this time overcoming France 55–35 in a Super Saturday Six Nations finale which had 12 sizzling tries; England once more, edging past hot favourites New Zealand in the 2019 World Cup semi-final in Japan, judged by many to be the best game of the tournament.

What about that day in Dublin when Ireland were agonisingly defeated 22–24 by the All Blacks with the clock in the red, a highly emotionally-charged afternoon at the Aviva Stadium as it was the last chance for those true Irish legends, Brian O'Driscoll and Paul O'Connell, to beat the All Blacks. Cue broken hearts everywhere.

It was a pleasure to be involved in such sporting spectacles, but I'd also like to think I played my own part to a degree in 'managing' the games. The easiest thing in the world to do as a referee is blow your whistle, the difficult part is knowing when not to. Having empathy for the game and the teams involved is arguably even more important. I was confident in my ability to make the correct calls because, unlike years earlier, I was now comfortable in my own skin. I wasn't living a lie any more. That made me a better person and certainly a better referee.

Things just snowballed. I refereed seven Heineken European Cup finals, club rugby's biggest game and our equivalent of the UEFA Champions League, including three on the trot. That was some honour. There were also further Euro finals in the Challenge Cup, the next level down, and six Guinness PRO14 finals. None of this, and I do mean none of it, would have been possible had I not accepted who I was.

Which brings me back to the tear-jerking letter from Devon. The mum of this teenage boy went on to explain how one night they had friends around for dinner and it was announced on TV that myself and my good friend Wayne Barnes, the English official, were going to referee at the World Cup.

One of the other dads asked, 'Isn't Nigel Owens the gay referee?'

To which the kid's own dad replied, 'Yes, but it doesn't matter what his sexuality is. Provided he's good at refereeing and deserves to go, that's the only thing that matters.'

The letter went on to say that their son heard this, popped upstairs, Googled my name, read previous reports of why I tried to take my own life, and the following morning plucked up the courage to tell his mum and dad, 'I've got something to tell you. The reason why I tried to take my own life is same reason why Nigel Owens did. I think I'm gay.'

His parents were somewhat shocked, but his dad said, 'It doesn't matter, we love you.'

In her beautiful letter to me, the mum explained that her boy had taken inspiration from my own story, it gave him the courage he needed to be himself, and she thanked me for sharing it with people. 'Thanks to role models like you we realised we can get on with life, be a family again and my son can now accept who he is and knows that we still love him no matter what,' she wrote.

Let me tell you right here, right now, that letter, which I have kept, means more to me than anything I have done on a rugby field. Yes, I feel incredibly privileged for the career I've had, refereeing so many epic games, truly world-class players, and at some of the finest sporting amphitheatres on the planet. However, I hope I will be remembered more perhaps for helping to break down barriers and making it a little bit easier for others to be themselves, not only in society and everyday life, but also in whatever sport they choose to participate in. That, and rugby proving to be truly a sport for all, is more important to me than even the World Cup final. It really is.

Do you know, I've never watched that 2015 Twickenham final between the All Blacks and the Wallabies since, but

I've read and re-read that letter from the relieved mum because it meant a life had been saved.

I had a similar reaction from many after appearing on the flagship BBC Radio 4 show *Desert Island Discs* to talk about how I came through my own dark days. The presenter Kirsty Young, who I'd been open and honest with during the programme about my struggles, leaned across at the end and said, 'Wow, that's special Nigel. We've done a few of these over the years and this one is going to help so many people out there. You'll be amazed at the response you'll get from this.' I thanked her for making me feel so comfortable opening up on something very personal and emotional. Her interviewing style was so caring, yet efficient. A wonderful person.

Kirsty was right, too. People still stop me in the street and say how much they loved that particular show, how it moved them to tears, how it has helped loved ones they know. I can't really put into words how much that means to me.

When I reflect upon my own initial fears, and look back at how rugby accepted me so readily, this sport of big, strong, powerful alpha males, it's truly humbling. The night before that World Cup final, BBC One showed a documentary called *Nigel Owens: True to Himself*, where my early troubles were charted. When the final whistle blew at Twickenham, one of the first things All Blacks flanker Jerome Kaino did was come up to shake my hand. 'Thanks Nige ...' he started '... And I watched your documentary last night. I don't think you'll ever know how much good that will have done, how much you help people inside and outside of rugby.'

Wow, this true hard-man of the game – well you had to be hard to play in that All Blacks pack – had just won the

World Cup and yet here he was taking the trouble to tell me that. To me that underlines how truly special our game is. Rugby can certainly learn from other sports, be it football, cricket, boxing, whatever, but I am convinced we lead the way on values, respect, diversity, fair play and inclusiveness. I'm probably living proof of that.

That's not to say there haven't been examples of bigotry. There are in all walks of life. I was refereeing England's 21–24 defeat to New Zealand at Twickenham in the autumn of 2014 when, unbeknown to me at the time, a couple of fans directed homophobic abuse towards me. This only came to light when another English supporter by the name of Keith Wilson, a straight man in his 60s and who was also at the game, wrote a letter to the *Guardian* newspaper expressing his disgust at comments he heard from those sitting nearby. He wrote about being horrified that 'a bunch of men half my age watching a rugby match in the 21st century could be capable of hurling such nasty, foul-mouthed, racist, homophobic abuse at an openly gay match official' and went on to say he was 'ashamed to hear such vitriol'.

The Rugby Football Union launched an investigation and, because of the way the ticketing system worked, they were able to identify the two individuals who were later banned from England games for two years and had to pay £1,000 each to a charity of my choice. The former England and Lions captain Bill Beaumont, then chairman of the RFU, sent me a personal handwritten note to apologise, stressed they were horrified by what had happened, and made it clear that they would deal with it and assured me that I was most welcome at Twickenham any time.

That was an example of rugby rallying around, but for me Mr Wilson is the one who perhaps deserves most credit here. When people speak of barriers being broken down, and point to the likes of myself and Gareth Thomas, the ex-Wales and Lions skipper who also came out, I argue the person writing that letter to the newspaper did more for the cause than even we managed. Without his courage to speak out, nobody would have known about this. It would have been swept under the carpet and these individuals might have carried on with homophobic remarks. I always say that whilst we have a personal responsibility in what we say and do in life, we also have a duty to ensure we don't say and do nothing when we hear something that is blatantly discriminatory and wrong. This gentleman Keith Wilson certainly set the right example here.

To be fair, Twickenham, and indeed the Welsh Rugby Union, ran a 'No Bystanders' campaign, urging individuals to act if they heard unacceptable comments. Sometimes these things need to be self-policed.

Unfortunately, we couldn't nail down the perpetrator from another game, this time involving Llanelli and Neath in the Welsh Premiership – although I'm pretty confident quite a few knew exactly who it was, but for some reason would not come forward to call out the unacceptable and hurtful language directed my way. The Llanelli scrum-half Gareth Davies, who went on to win Lions selection, was lining up a match-winning kick at the end when we heard a Neath supporter shout very loudly, 'Owens, you gay so and so.' The stewards stepped in, we thought we'd identified the culprit, but were unable to prove definitively it was him. Again I received a lovely letter, this time from the chairman of Neath, apologising for what had happened and emphasising that I was always welcome down at The Gnoll.

I must stress though, these examples stand out because of their rarity. Yes, family and friends tell me occasionally of things they hear said about me at matches, but crikey as a referee you're never going to be Mr Popular. Abuse goes with the territory, normally coming from the supporters of the team that is losing, but there's a world of difference between rugby criticism, or banter, and downright homophobia.

My general experience is one of a sport where 99 per cent of those involved rallied around me. Then you get letters like the one I received from the Exeter mum, which puts everything into an even sharper focus. Someone's life has to be more important than any game of rugby, even a World Cup final, does it not?

I could even see the funny side when I took my godson and little cousins to watch a European Cup game between the Scarlets and French aristocrats Racing 92 in Llanelli the day after I'd refereed a gripping Saracens versus Toulouse clash at Wembley on the Friday night. Evidently unhappy with the way the match was going, a home supporter shouted out, 'This ref is bent'.

'No, that's Nigel Owens. He was reffing last night,' someone else responded.

I was sitting two rows back. This spectator's face was a picture when, having been informed by others of my nearby presence, he turned around to indeed see it was me. Red-faced, embarrassed, full of contrition, he said, 'Nigel, I'm so sorry. I didn't mean it in a nasty way at all.'

I knew full well he didn't, too. I'd got the context in which he meant his remark, more a funny, joking manner than being horrible. 'It's OK, no problem,' I replied. 'By the way, I may be bent off the field, but I'm as straight as they come on it!'

Everyone laughed and we got on with watching the game. Typically, the youngsters with me, Dion, Sion, Ioan and Elis, thought it was the best moment of the day!

As my own story became more well known, and talk grew of me potentially refereeing a World Cup final, things just kind of exploded and I guess a big part of that included how clips of my interactions with players during matches began to go viral on social media. Unbeknown to me, I must stress, and most certainly unintentionally, because I definitely didn't use such expressions to court publicity.

The most famous of these, I guess, was when I lectured an Italian player for incessant backchat, ending with the words, 'This is Not Soccer.' One of the great strengths of rugby union is the respect shown to the referee, how dissent is not tolerated, and I never want to see that creep in. Around that time there was a huge debate in the media about backchat to referees in football and, looking back, I suppose that was why I used those particular words. In my own mind, though, I was simply doing my job as a referee to control a rugby game. I had absolutely no idea it would court this type of publicity, even being mentioned on *Match of the Day* one Saturday night.

No-one was more shocked at the reaction than me. Apparently, people commented on how hilarious my words had been. They were hardly that funny, surely? I didn't think so, anyway.

Same when, during the World Cup final, the great All Blacks Number 10 Dan Carter stood next to me and told me he was 'f****d', and I replied, 'Shhh, don't swear now, you're on telly mun.' How was I to know that was going to have thousands upon thousands of YouTube views or, even more bizarre, that T-shirts of the comment would be made? It was just me being me, urging Carter to be cautious because as referee I was obviously mic'd up and I didn't want his words beamed into front rooms throughout the world where youngsters might be watching.

I ended up sending one of those T-shirts to Dan. A few weeks after that Twickenham final a parcel arrived at my home. It was a framed photograph of Carter standing next to me and lining up one of his kicks that afternoon. He'd written on the back, 'To Nigel, Don't Swear Now, You're On Telly Man – Congrats on a great refereeing career – Dan Carter.' That was a lovely touch from a great man and a great player.

Because of all this social media attention, and the backdrop of how I managed to reach the top of my profession, people latched on to it and thus fame – and awards – began to follow. I was given the MBE, presented to me by His Royal Highness Prince William. I was named 'Gay Sports Personality of the Decade' at the Stonewall awards ceremony in London. That one was presented to me by the legendary actor Sir Ian McKellen, star of movies such as *The Lord of the Rings*, *X-Men* and *The Hobbit*. He told me he'd watched the World Cup final in a pub full of Kiwis and Australians cheering on their respective teams. 'Myself and my partner were the only two shouting for the referee!' Sir Ian smiled.

Attitude, the UK's best-selling gay magazine, named me 'Most Influential Sports Person of the Year' in 2017. I received the First Minister's Special Award from the Welsh Government for helping to break down barriers. There were even online petitions for me to be named BBC Wales Sports Personality of the Year, until the organisers pointed out that a referee couldn't be classed as a sports competitor. So they gave me a Special Achievement award instead.

There are five university doctorates and various other honours, too. I did not set out to win these, but there's obviously a sense of pride that people think highly enough of you and give you awards for what you've done not only in rugby, but also for LGBT rights, mental health awareness – which I'm heavily involved with – and my work with the charity BulliesOut, something I also feel extremely strongly about.

I kind of became a victim of my own success in a way I suppose, because I wasn't courting any of this. But do you know, another beauty of our wonderful sport of rugby is that someone, somewhere, even in the most unlikely of quarters, will always make sure you never get too big for your boots; your feet remain firmly planted on the ground.

High-profile referee or not, one Sunday morning I'd dashed back to Wales after taking charge of a big Heineken European Cup match at Leicester's Welford Road, having promised to do an under-12s game between Pencoed and Cwmbran the next day. The community game, to me, is the most important part of rugby; without it none of us could get to the top level, and I always try to put something back in at grassroots level. The young players, team officials and watching parents were evidently delighted I'd agreed to do the match. They gave me a lovely warm welcome, the players' faces were a picture as they had no idea I was turning up. 'It's Nigel Owens, we can't believe you're going to referee our game!' they said.

Then came the line that well and truly put me in my place. One of the youngsters piped up, 'Yes, thanks for coming

Nigel ... but I hope you're going to referee this match better than you did last night's!'

Ouch. That was me well and truly told. But this is what rugby is all about. Banter, respect and a true love of the game. No matter how old you are, or whatever your background.

CHAPTER TWO

Dark days, seeing the light

I SOMETIMES WONDER, with the way society has changed in becoming far more inclusive, how a young Nigel Owens would have reacted today to the many struggles I faced during my late teens, through my twenties and indeed early thirties, before things thankfully took off for me. I can't say for 100 per cent certain, but my guess is that it would have been very different. I'd probably have accepted my sexuality a bit sooner, thus avoiding the dark, dark place I was in back then as I did everything I could not to be gay – including trying to take my own life.

What you have to remember though is that 25 to 30 years ago things were very different to modern-day Britain. For a proper insight into the demons that were going through my mind back then, let's rewind to the 1970s for a moment and go on a little journey with me to see what things were like back in the day.

I was brought up in the small west Wales village of Mynyddcerrig, about 15 miles north-west of Swansea, an old-fashioned coal mining and rural community. Indeed, my dad Geraint was a miner and quarry worker at the local limestone quarry. There were only 140 people in the village and every household was fluent in the Welsh language. Your upbringing defines you: my parents taught me to say please and thank you, the value of respect – good habits I'd like to think I still possess today. The expectation for me was, like that of any other boy I suppose, that I'd get a girlfriend, then get married, and my mum and dad would become proud grandparents. It was the way of the world.

Except, in my late teens I noticed I was becoming attracted to men, something alien to me. I was becoming somebody I didn't want to be. I wasn't fitting in with what I thought my mum and dad wanted from me. For all the excellent strides made by the LGBT community, just put yourself in my position briefly. Every word used to describe a gay person had an element of either nastiness or negativity about it: poof, homo, faggot. Even these days you'll hear youngsters saying, 'I don't like school, it's gay.' Nothing horrible is meant by it, but the connotations are negative and it hurts to hear that.

So I'd be sitting on the sofa with my mum and dad, watching TV programmes containing the odd stereotypical and very camp character, like the one played by John Inman on *Are You Being Served*? I spent a lot of time on my own just to get away from that environment. This, no doubt, led me to not be as close to my friends as I would have been had I been leading a normal life like them. I was so scared of being found out, I just couldn't risk being in their company too often. Every time I heard any of them mention the word gay, my stomach would churn with fear. I'd feel sick, scared, alone.

I started comfort eating: kebabs, chips, takeaways, chocolate. I wasn't in good shape, overweight at 16½ stone, and struggled to keep up with the players I was refereeing.

That's when the bulimia struck. I ate a lot, drank a lot, but to stop becoming fat I'd bring it all back up eight or nine times a day, week after week, month after month, year after year. I went down to 10½ stone, looked very pale, gaunt and unwell.

What did I do next? I over-compensated by going to the gym to put on muscle. Well, you know what they say about gay people taking extra pride in their appearance. I needed to do something if other men were to find me attractive. That's when I started using steroids, and became hooked on them. Invariably, they were causing side effects, making me feel even worse. This was a kind of Perfect Storm, chicken and the egg, and it wasn't good.

By the time I was 25 I was in a dark place. Very depressed. The suicidal thoughts were getting more frequent. The bulimia and steroids were symptoms, but the main cause was that I was gay, somebody I didn't want to be. I read an article in a newspaper saying that being gay was not only morally wrong, it was also something you could be cured from. The cure was being chemically castrated! How naive could I be? However, anything that could help me get better, such was my mindset.

Off I went to the doctor's surgery. 'Look, I think I might be gay. I don't want to be gay and I've read there is a cure, so can I get chemically castrated?'

He looked me straight in the eye. 'Nigel, it doesn't work like that. You are who you are.'

The doctor continued, 'This is not your answer. Instead, I can put you in touch with someone to talk to about it.' Trouble was, I didn't want to talk to anyone, not even qualified medical professionals. I couldn't risk it in case I'd get found out. It had already taken months and months of sleepless nights and anguish to pluck up the courage to actually go and see the doctor in the first place.

I left his surgery in an even worse state of mind than before, found myself in a deeper and deeper hole. The suicidal thoughts became stronger. Then, one night, I did the thing I will always regret most in my life, something I will never, ever forgive myself for. In the early hours I left a goodbye note for my mum and dad, telling them that I loved them very much and was so sorry for any pain I'd caused. I didn't tell them why, but said in the note I couldn't carry on living my life any more.

I walked a few miles to where my dad was born, the small farm of Moultan on the back roads of the village, and looked at all those places where I'd had such happy childhood memories. Then I headed to the place where Dewi Morgan, who I'd helped out on the farm and always felt part of the family, had taken his own life a few years earlier. I couldn't end it there, it didn't seem right to bring back those memories to his daughters and other family members I was close to. So, instead, I headed up the Banc-y-ddraenen mountainside right above our house, armed with pills, a bottle of whisky and a shotgun – which I had because I used to work on the farm and did a bit of shooting, mostly rabbits which my mum would then cook and we'd have for dinner.

I'll never forgive myself for the pain and worry I put my parents through that night, and indeed for years afterwards, leaving them wondering if I would ever try to do it again. Perhaps that's why that lovely letter I received from the Exeter mum, thanking me for saving her own boy's life, had such a forceful impact on me.

Back on the mountain I overdosed, slipped into a coma,

and strangely enough that actually saved my life. Had I not done so, make no mistake, I would have pulled the trigger. That I have no doubt of. My mum, having seen the note I left, alerted the authorities; police, family and friends were out looking for me on that cold, damp, miserable morning. Heat sensors from the police helicopter detected me. I was airlifted to West Wales General Hospital, put into intensive care and, as I came around the doctor told me, 'Nigel, you're a very, very lucky young man. Another 20 minutes ...'

To everyone involved in finding and saving me that day, I can never thank you enough. I will always, always, be in your debt. Needless to say, none of what I went on to achieve as a referee at the very highest level would have been possible without their concern and help.

As you can imagine, I had lots of visitors in the hospital. Then, one night, after the others had left, my mum came back in on her own, sat by my bedside, held my hand and said, 'Listen Nigel, if you do anything like that again, then you might as well take me and your dad with you. We can't and don't want to carry on our own lives without you.' We cried together as I sat on the bed, mum in the chair next to me. That night I realised I simply couldn't continue like this any more. I needed to be more honest with myself and those close to me. This is who I am, I have no choice in the matter. You can choose many things in life, your car, house, where to go out in the evening, which football team to support, what sport to play. But not your sexuality. You are who you are. There *is* no choice. I needed to somehow understand and come to terms with that.

Let me tell you something. Refereeing that World Cup final between Australia and New Zealand, the biggest game in world rugby which happens only every four years, was a hugely pressurised occasion. You're in front of 85,000 people at Twickenham and millions watching around the world, with 40 different cameras in the stadium ensuring each single decision you make is scrutinised from every possible angle. You dare not get it wrong – in many ways the world is on your shoulders. Yet that was nothing, trust me when I say absolutely nothing, compared to the challenge of accepting who I truly was.

That's the same for anybody with the sort of demons I was wrestling with. Unless you accept yourself, or indeed accept there are issues you need to deal with, whatever those may be, then you cannot go on to the next stage of what to do about it. You can only enjoy your life, your work, be the best you can be, by being yourself – and being allowed to be yourself, too. You cannot live a lie. Once I finally did that, life improved and my refereeing got better and better. These could never have happened – not the World Cup, not the 100 Tests, not the big club Cup finals – until I actually started to be honest with myself.

I still kept it a secret for another few years, until I was in my mid-thirties. Well, no-one had come out in public in the macho world of rugby. How could I? This sport of big, strong, powerful alpha males, with all that famous and indeed notorious rugby dressing room banter. I was in constant, stomach churning fear of people finding out about me. It was affecting my refereeing. Again, I just knew this couldn't carry on.

One of the triggers for change was a game I refereed between Japan and Ireland in Osaka in the summer of 2005. Not particularly well either, as Paddy O'Brien, the International Rugby Board referees' manager at the time, quite rightly told me. In fact he really laid it on the line. That autumn there were 18 referees, but only 17 international matches, so something, or someone, had to give. 'You were the worst performer Nigel,' said Paddy. Nothing held back there, then. But Paddy was right and I knew it. No prizes for guessing who was the unfortunate one to miss out. I thought that's it, my career is over and my job is on the line now too, as one of the provisos for being a professional referee was you would become, and continue to be, an international official.

Then, quite out of the blue, I received another phone call from Paddy which was to change my life. An 18th game had suddenly been arranged for the beginning of December between Argentina and Western Samoa. I was handed an 11th-hour reprieve, but very much on the proviso that if I didn't perform better this time, I would never do another Test match.

I had three months to get myself right. Physically, I was fit as a fiddle, mentally I was still struggling badly. Do I carry on living a lie and not doing my job properly as a result, or do I give up a job that I love because I can't stop living a lie and don't want people to find out? The burden of living every day in constant fear of being found out was affecting me badly, both on and off the field.

None of us should be presented with that choice, but I did, and indeed people still do today. I chose neither option. I decided it was time to be honest. It took me three and a half hours to tell my mum, the very person, with my dad, I trusted more than anyone else. We cried together once more, and then she told me, 'Nigel, nothing changes between us. You are my son and I will always love and support you. But you need to understand things will change for you from now on and it might be difficult at times.'

She was right, too.

'Oh … and you need to tell your dad.'

Mum had kind of guessed anyway. In the end she was the one who broke the news to my dad. He was shocked and shaken a bit at first, but his support for me throughout my career, attending matches and sticking up for his son amid any criticism, has been unwavering. As I write these words dad is now 87 years of age, still loves me the same, nothing's changed. How lucky I've been to have such wonderful, understanding parents.

Next I had to tell Bob Yeman, the Welsh Rugby Union's referees' manager. I needed to learn whether I could come out and still be a referee. He too was incredibly supportive, as were senior officials, and indeed everybody at the WRU and in rugby in general. I owe so much to them all for their backing at the time and continued support since, right through to this day.

A truly massive weight had been lifted from my shoulders. I flew out to Buenos Aires for that Argentina–Western Samoa game a different person, in a much more relaxed frame of mind. The constant fear, being scared of being found out, had gone. I was happy, just enjoying being myself. I didn't shout it from the rooftops, but if anyone asked I didn't have to lie any more.

As I walked out of the mouth of the tunnel and crossed the white touchline onto the field, I said something to myself which I've repeated for every single game since: Whatever you do, don't f*** it up.

I refereed that game well. I had a great review and Paddy was very happy. It was the springboard. Just four matches on, I was doing England versus Italy in front of a packed house at Twickenham, the first of a record 21 Six Nations matches for any referee. All those other historic games were to follow at club and country level. I don't wish to labour the point, but I would never have done any of them had I not accepted who I was. A happy referee is a good referee.

As for my fears about the macho world of rugby? Not long afterwards my secret was laid bare in front of everybody after I did a TV interview about being a gay referee, which was later picked up by newspapers ranging from *The Sun* to my local paper, the *Carmarthen Journal*.

This was to be another acid test – how would players, and indeed supporters, react to my news? Shortly afterwards I was doing fitness work in Swansea, where the Ospreys also had their training base, and their skipper Barry Williams, the Wales and Lions hooker, came up to shake me by the hand. He looked me in the eye and told me he had huge respect for what I'd done. I'd been very brave and being gay would make absolutely no difference to him or the other players. That broke the ice, I guess. Rugby quickly allowed me to be who I am.

That should be the case in any workplace, quite frankly. It shouldn't matter who you are, what your sexual orientation is, colour of skin or creed is, everyone in society should be treated the same. No better or worse, none of this ticking of boxes we sometimes see in today's society. Just simply the same.

Because I'm involved with mental health charities, I get asked to attend functions and talk a lot about my own emotional journey. It's not an easy thing to do, spilling it out in front of lots of people you don't even know, but if my story helps just one person in that room, then it's worth it in my eyes.

Other role models in sport have started to be more open,

and that also is bound to help. Dame Kelly Holmes, our wonderful double gold medal winning Olympic champion, came out as gay in the summer of 2022 after saying she'd hidden her secret for more than 30 years. When I read Kelly's heart-rending interview as she spoke of her fears, her suicidal thoughts and finally her need to stop living a lie and to be herself, it brought back so many memories of a younger version of me.

I have nothing but the most enormous admiration for the young Blackpool footballer Jake Daniels, the UK's first active male player to come out publicly as gay in the world's most popular sport. I do lots of talks during Mental Health Awareness week and one of the questions I'm invariably asked in the customary Q&A sessions that follow afterwards is, 'Why do no footballers admit to being gay?'

Everyone has been waiting to find out who the first Premier League star will be. My reply is always the same: 'It's a matter of when, not if.' Until Jake chose to 'break the stigma', his words not mine, footballers had been reluctant to come out for fear of discrimination, chants from opposition supporters on the terraces and the effect this could have on themselves and their team.

But I always say at these Q&A sessions that, just like in rugby, the vast majority of people in football are very decent human beings and would be supportive of any player in such circumstances. We're seeing that already with young Jake; football authorities, lots of different clubs and major household names such as Gary Lineker, have rallied around him. I'd like to think that if there's the odd offensive chant from opposition fans at matches, they will be drowned out by the much greater numbers supporting Jake.

What his case has already done is take away the excuse

about uncertainty over how football would handle such a scenario. Football *has* accepted it. We've already seen that with the support Jake is receiving, yet there could still be reticence from others just because of the global nature of the sport. Would a world-renowned footballer, a global superstar, really be prepared to come out when he knew the news would be on the front and back pages of pretty much every newspaper on the planet? Would he want to be that first major person? I'm not sure. It's taken long enough even at the lower level of the game, but what I'm convinced about is that while Jake is the first, he certainly won't be the last.

As for myself, I've still had to battle the bulimia on and off, even ahead of selection for the 2015 World Cup when as referees we were expected to reach an incredibly high level of fitness. I'd finally managed to stop it after a very significant and sad occasion in my life, when my mum was diagnosed with terminal cancer in 2007. That hit me badly. I spent the day comfort eating and felt bloated, but on this occasion I just couldn't bring the food back up no matter how much I tried. I realised then it was silly making myself unwell, when my mum had no choice and was now going to fight every day against an illness that she could do nothing about. So, just like that, the bulimia stopped. For several years. Then, ahead of the World Cup, it was back, triggered by the pressures of needing to pass a fitness test. Now, don't get me wrong, if you want to referee at the highest level then you have to be fit. If not, you simply won't last. But the level they were expecting from us, and remember I was in my forties, was more than some rugby players needed to achieve.

We had to do something called a Yo-Yo test, a variation

of the beep test which involves running between cones the length of a cricket pitch and doing it faster each time to beat the beep. We were told we needed to reach a figure of 18.1 – crikey, some of the players don't get to that.

I was the oldest referee at the tournament, yet I was told I had to hit that mark. That put an awful lot of pressure on me and I slipped back into my old habit of comfort eating, and thinking that making myself sick after food would help me shed some kilograms. Trust me, it was tough trying to hide that, but thanks to my strength and conditioning coach at the WRU, I was the fittest I'd ever been. I passed the test. The bulimia was still there throughout the tournament, but no-one else knew.

Of all the games I've refereed, I've never been found wanting on fitness. However, there was also a bit of a trend starting which I've never agreed with. Some appeared to be putting too much emphasis on having referees who looked like the players, were as fit, or even fitter, than them, as opposed to referees who could actually officiate the game properly. I said this to a fellow referee once who made a point of letting me know that his fitness test results were way ahead of mine. My reply was a simple one. 'There's no point getting to the breakdown if you haven't got a f*****g clue what to do when you get there, is there.'

If you're not fit it will show in your performances, but if you're refereeing well and on top of your game, then how fit you actually are, or how you look, won't matter. Interestingly, before the 2019 World Cup there was no fitness testing for selection, apart from what we did with our own fitness gurus at our respective unions, with a personal goal tailored to each of us. I suspect they knew deep down that if they put in another cut-off point, as in 2015, then myself and the Frenchman Jérôme Garcès would not have made it to Japan. Yet Jérôme got the final, and I refereed the England versus New Zealand semi-final. We were told by some on the selection panel that we were the two best referees at the tournament. So while fitness and image has its place, it should never become the be-all and end-all of refereeing.

Sadly, my mum passed away in 2009 after her battle with cancer, so unfortunately she never got to see my career take off in the way it did. She was the person who gave me the most support during those dark days, held my hand, shared the tears, offered the best advice, insisted upon unconditional love.

But I'd like to think she was looking down on me that day I refereed the World Cup final, and indeed on many of the other big matches I was given the privilege of refereeing. I couldn't have done any of this without her backing. She'd have been immensely proud of what her once deeply troubled, but always beloved son went on to achieve.

Thanks mum.

CHAPTER THREE

This is not soccer and the odd Twitter spat

'COME HERE. TIME out please. I don't think we've met before, but I'm the referee on this field, not you. Stick to your job and I will do mine. If I hear you shouting for *anything* again, I'm going to be penalising you. This is Not Soccer, is that clear? Back you go and get on with your game.'

When I uttered those seemingly innocuous words to the 22-times capped Italy scrum-half Tobias Botes, who was playing for Treviso against Munster at Thomond Park in Limerick, I had absolutely no idea they would go viral. None whatsoever. This was simply a case of me, as the referee, dealing with what I saw as dissent on the field of play.

Such is the age of social media. I'm told a video of the incident has been shared so often that it's had more than two million views on YouTube. I find that staggering. There are also compilations to be found of my so-called one-liners to players which people have apparently found funny. Nigel Owens quotes and compilations? Come on, are they really that amusing? I certainly didn't think so at the time. Nor do I now, to be perfectly honest.

However, given the power and reach of the internet, I

guess a mix of the above, refereeing a World Cup final, being the first person to come out in rugby, talking publicly about LGBT, mental health and other life issues, plus appearances on TV shows, does make me a bit of a celebrity in the eyes of some people.

Frankly, it's not something I particularly think a great deal about, but I suppose I can't deny that I'm well known. I do get recognised and asked for autographs when walking down the street or on the Tube whenever I visit London, or even on the M4 when a passing motorist will do a double take, then beep their horn.

The recognition is nice, of course it is, and I always try to help out if members of the public want a selfie or an autograph. However, whatever category of celebrity people choose to put me in – C list, D list, even Z list, but most certainly not A or B – the most important thing is that it has happened through me simply being who I am, not because I have actively sought fame. I certainly didn't announce I was gay, or talk about my past problems and eating disorders, in order to become a celebrity. I was just being honest with myself, and if my experiences help others deal with similar traumas to those I went through, then I'm comfortable with that.

I was on the stage doing stand-up comedy at 14 years of age, and acting on kids' programmes on the Welsh TV channel S4C a year before that. That's just who I am, who I've always been. Yes, I'm active on Twitter, I've got more than 425,000 followers, but I like engaging with people, just as others do on social media.

What's wrong with that? It's a great platform for debate – or for me to explain refereeing decisions at times. I certainly don't say things on there to get noticed, for something to go viral, be picked up by the media, or to increase my fame. That's not me.

To that end I've never once – and I do mean never – gone out onto a rugby pitch with a pre-prepared line thinking, if I say something clever and funny it will get loads of hits, likes and comments on the internet. No, I've just done what comes naturally to me as a referee, tried to manage a game properly, implement the rules. My philosophy has always been that I'm there to referee a game of rugby for the players to the best of my ability, nothing more and nothing less. The truth is I'm more shocked than anyone when others deem my comments, one-liners, whatever you wish to call them, to be so funny they end up going viral.

Which brings us back to Mr Botes and 'This is Not Soccer' as Munster beat Treviso 29–11 in a PRO12 game I was officiating at the beginning of January 2012. Let me explain exactly how that happened. There had been a bit of a hoo-ha over gamesmanship after the 2010 football World Cup in South Africa, plenty of chatter in the media about players rolling around, diving to try to con the referee into giving a penalty, or running up and surrounding him to complain about decisions.

This is not a case of rugby taking the moral high ground over soccer – we have issues of our own that need addressing, make no mistake about that – but there were concerns that that kind of thing was starting to creep into rugby where respect for the referee has historically been sacrosanct and must always remain so. It should never be a case of the referee is never wrong – although there is a famous saying that a referee is always right. Ha! However, respect on the field must not be eroded or the game is finished.

Now, I'd not refereed Treviso for a few years and pretty

early on I noticed their scrum-half was moaning about my decisions, gesturing, waving his arms in the air. The first thing that went through my mind was, Hang on a minute, I don't think I've refereed this guy before. If I had, I felt he'd have known better than to be acting like this.

I let it go for a little while, but when I awarded Munster a scrum for a turnover, after their excellent and inspirational captain Paul O'Connell had held up the ball in a maul, Botes started complaining about the Irishman not releasing. I'd had enough. I blew my whistle, called Botes and his captain Antonio Pavanello over for a word.

'The law is quite clear, the maul is formed, held up, unplayable, turnover ball, no issues whatsoever,' I explained to the skipper.

Then I turned to Botes. I didn't think I'd refereed him previously, I started, before making it clear I wanted him to accept my decisions without complaining all the time – and I guess the 'This is Not Soccer' line came to me spontaneously as part of that because there had been so much talk about backchat in the round ball game.

I certainly wasn't aware that the TV commentator said at the time, 'Well, that told him ... and if Tobias Botes hasn't met Nigel Owens before, he has now.' Yes, it was a bit of a ticking-off, but to me it was no more than a referee exerting his authority because I didn't want that kind of dissent coming into rugby.

Lecture handed out, I thought absolutely nothing more of it. Botes was well behaved for the rest of the match, and the message I'd tried to give seemed to have been received. So it came as a shock immediately afterwards when my TMO (Television Match Official) Seamus Flannery approached me as I was sitting down in the changing room and said,

'Nige, we were laughing our heads off in the truck. My mates, my wife, the kids have all been texting "What Nigel said was brilliant". It's so funny it's already gone viral all over social media.'

I looked up at him perplexed, and responded, 'What do you mean viral? Why, what did I say?' I genuinely didn't know what he was on about, certainly not the significance of it, until I looked at my phone – and whoosh ... messages everywhere.

Fortunately, there was a positive response. My comments even merited a mention on *Match of the Day* as pundits discussed the differing respect for referees in the two sports, while leading football columnists on the top national newspapers wrote articles to say they wished more of this happened in their sport and players listened to officials more instead of moaning. I was perplexed by the reaction, or perhaps that should be over-reaction? Crikey, a clothing company from Italy even contacted me to ask if I'd mind them using my image next to the words 'This is Not Soccer' on T-shirts. They thought it was a great slogan and a commercial opportunity, mystifying me even further.

A few months later I was back in Ireland, this time refereeing a Leinster game, when I noticed eight youngsters sat together in the stands all had the said T-shirts on. They'd clearly worn them because they knew I was doing the match and shouted out to ask if they could have a picture with me afterwards. Of course I replied, it would be my pleasure.

They evidently thought what I'd told Botes was funny, too. Yet I come back to it, I just said what came naturally to me at the time – and, to be fair to Botes, I had no trouble from him or his Italian team-mates for the rest of the game, which, as I say, was the sole intention.

Football started to become something of a theme, I suppose, because two more incidents were to follow which also went viral. The first was in a Heineken Cup match between Leicester and Ulster at Welford Road in 2014 when the home team's England centre Anthony Allen started complaining after I'd penalised him for holding on. Everything seemed to be OK, Ulster's Ruan Pienaar had even started to line up his kick at goal, but I was just semi-mindful of Allen carping on about it a few yards away. Once again I blew my whistle, walked towards him and said, again totally spontaneously, 'Hey, the football stadium is 500 yards that way.'

That, of course, was a reference to Leicester City's King Power Stadium being just down the road, the venue where they were to win their fairytale Premier League title a couple of years on. Once more I didn't think anything of my remark, there was still plenty of chatter at the time about a lack of respect towards referees in football and it was clearly on my mind, but once again when I came off the pitch I was told a video clip was already going viral.

'Do people really think that's so funny?' I asked friends, because I certainly didn't think so. Allen, like Botes in that previous game, didn't protest much after I spoke to him. So once again the message I was attempting to get across had been received and accepted, which was the only aim.

Same with an incident involving Stuart Hogg at the 2015 World Cup, another one that had a ridiculous number of shares and likes on social media. Scotland were playing South Africa in a Pool B decider at Newcastle United's iconic St James' Park Premier League stadium. Football, and the venue, was clearly on my mind again because when Hogg took a bit of a theatrical dive to the floor, I wasn't impressed. Hogg was clearing from his own 22 when he was brushed, at most, by Springbok prop Tendai 'The Beast' Mtawarira, who was attempting to charge down the kick. I knew the challenge was legal and next time the ball went out of play I ran straight over to Hogg to tell him, 'He was committed in the air, there was nothing wrong with that. Dive like that again and come back here in two weeks to play, not today. Watch it.'

Newcastle were playing Norwich at St James' in a fortnight and again, in my eyes, it was merely a reference to some of the play-acting that can blight football and I was letting Hogg know what he did wasn't acceptable. I don't know why I uttered those particular words, maybe I'd watched a few football games beforehand and saw attempts to con the referee which annoyed me. Whatever, once more I merely said what came naturally at the time. Scotland's captain Greig Laidlaw, who was listening in, was grinning. Hogg started giggling to himself a little, accepting the rebuke and admitting he was wrong.

For whatever reason, once more people found my comment amusing. The TV commentator laughed and said, 'Quote of the World Cup – and it's come from a referee. Nigel Owens again showing who's boss.' It wasn't about that, it was about ensuring the values of our great game were being properly respected and upheld. To be fair to Stuart, nobody knows those values better than him. He has gone on to have a fabulous career as a truly world-class full-back, a brilliant captain of Scotland and a well deserved British and Irish Lion.

I've never had any trouble from him since, and in any case I knew at the time, as once more the incident went viral and people started to make a fuss on social media, that I'd have had the full support of a rather important ally in the shape of Stuart's dad, John Hogg. I'm not sure how commonly known this is, but Hogg senior also used to be a rugby referee and was a touch judge for me at one of my first matches in charge up in Scotland when the Borders were playing – with little Stuart, then very young, on the side of the pitch watching! I guess he was destined to fall in love with the game and become a great player, even then.

I suppose those are among the Nigel Owens internet moments people talk about the most, but there have also been a few others which, again to my surprise, people also seem to enjoy sharing or watching on social media.

England versus France, an epic 2015 Six Nations showdown in front of more than 82,000 enthralled spectators at Twickenham which the Red Rose had to win by a margin of at least 26 points to snatch the Championship away from Ireland on what was known as Super Saturday. They gave it a right old go in a superb end-to-end, 12-try contest, but with nine minutes left, and leading 48–35 at the time, their captain Chris Robshaw was getting a little frustrated because he knew England were falling just a little short for the title.

Chris is a lovely guy, a super and often underrated player, a magnificent captain and wonderful ambassador for rugby. However, on this occasion, knowing England weren't quite there, he was in my ear a little bit too much when questioning a French player lying around at the base of a ruck in what he thought was an offside position. I had no problem with Chris querying things at first, and explained the player had moved, so no offence had taken place. Robshaw queried that again, pointed back to where the incident had taken place, and at this point I just raised my eyebrows a little and said in a stricter tone of voice, 'Err, Christopher'.

I don't know why I said Christopher, rather than Chris. It just happened. I suppose it's the kind of thing a lot of us get from our parents when growing up, realising we've done something wrong when our full name is suddenly used. In my case, instead of Nige it became Nigel, with some emphasis thrown in by my mum or dad. Or in Robshaw's case it would have been Christopher. You know then enough is enough, you've crossed the line.

This particular moment just all happened so fast. Robshaw tapped me on the arm and said 'Sorry sir', before backing off like the gentleman that he is.

'Thank you,' I responded.

Given that I simply spoke in that manner because I wanted Robshaw to accept my decision as the referee, which in the end he did, I was startled at the fallout as it went viral once more. People in England seem to love it; they bring me photographs of a husband, brother, uncle, cousin, or mate called Chris and ask me to sign it 'Err, Christopher' so they can give it as a present to their loved one. I've even had some asking me to pretend to dish out a red card whilst saying 'Err Christopher', so they can video it.

Yet at the time this was just a referee talking to a captain who had taken things slightly too far in the heat of a Test match battle in front of a passionate Twickenham crowd, with the Six Nations title on the line. To be fair to Robshaw, it was also most out of character. He wears his heart on his sleeve, nothing wrong with that, but is normally so respectful. A very genuine guy who I have so much admiration for. While he's not ranked as highly as Richie McCaw, David Pocock, Michael Hooper, Sam Warburton,

Justin Tipuric and other great openside flankers of his era, I always viewed Chris as a top-drawer rugby player in his own right. I saw his talents close up.

Unwittingly, Robshaw was also kind of involved in another one that did the rounds on social media, this time during a European Cup game between his club side Harlequins and Castres at the Twickenham Stoop. He caught a ball at the back of the lineout from a throw-in by Quins hooker Dave Ward which was perhaps the worst I've ever seen. It was so crooked Robshaw was almost in the scrum-half position by the time he clutched the catch and, as I blew my whistle, I think both sets of forwards were a little bit embarrassed, including Ward and Robshaw. No-one really wanted to say anything; even I was hesitating about asking Castres whether they wanted a scrum or lineout.

It was so quiet I thought I'd break the ice. 'I'm straighter than that one!' I said. Yet again spontaneous, on the spur of the moment, but it did the trick. Ward laughed, Robshaw grinned, everybody suddenly started smiling. Instead of players feeling awkward, we were able to just get on with the next phase of the game.

That was just me, in my own way, managing the moment as referee as I saw it in that particular instance, but what's important to stress is that I wasn't belittling Ward for his throw in any shape or form. I would never do that to any player, which is why the criticism I received from the former Ireland and Lions full-back Luke Fitzgerald, after Munster's hard-fought 10–7 Guinness PRO14 victory over Glasgow in 2017, annoyed me.

I was playing an advantage to Munster when their lock Billy Holland threw a bad pass into touch. He wasn't being challenged at the time, Munster had made ground, so I deemed advantage was over and awarded the lineout to Glasgow. This is how referees often judge if it's over or not; if we feel a player or team has made a poor decision, or execution of it, whilst not under undue pressure from the opposition at the time, then we call it over as it was their own doing.

Holland queried why play wasn't being brought back for the initial infringement and I explained, 'Advantage over there, lads. It's poor play by you there on the pass. Under no pressure there, advantage over.'

Fitzgerald went onto an Irish podcast to claim that I was being disrespectful to players, trying to be too smart and friendly, and needed to be anonymous as a referee. A newspaper headline about his comments read, 'There's no place for it in the game – Luke Fitzgerald calls on Nigel Owens to stop using witty put-downs.'

He also cited an incident at a Leinster versus Munster Irish derby clash a few months earlier when I'd told the home prop Cian Healy, 'The hands-out rule changed three years ago. Where have you been?' after he infringed at a ruck, knowing full well what he was doing.

Healy, a crafty front-row warrior with more than 100 Ireland caps to his name, jogged away with a smile on his face, knowing he'd been caught out and accepted my decision. Billy Holland also responded brilliantly to my comment to him by grinning, 'Cheers coach!' In fact, both players have mentioned to me since that they had no problem whatsoever with what I said and that they loved having me in charge of their games.

I'm all for constructive criticism of my decision-making as a referee when I get something wrong, but I felt Fitzgerald's remarks were unnecessary and I took to

Twitter to respond, making my views clear by saying, 'The game is about the players, not the ref. I didn't say a witty thing or a put-down. I just explained why advantage was over. Nothing more.'

Which is precisely what I was attempting to do. You can't have a double advantage; had a Glasgow player forced the error from Holland, then of course I'd have brought play back for the original offence, but that wasn't the case. I was trying to explain the situation to him, a referee communicating with the players so there was no question of doubt. There was certainly no attempt from me in the slightest to talk down to Holland and fortunately, as you can see, he took it in the right spirit, and told me later not to change my style of refereeing – and, indeed, admitted it was a bad pass!

Fitzgerald's criticism, and my response, sparked a big debate on social media. To be fair to him, Fitzgerald then responded: 'Nigel Owens – great ref, agree to disagree on comments made during games. Just my opinion, best of luck for the rest of the season.' However, I do wonder sometimes, though I'm not necessarily saying so in this case, do people deliberately say things about me because they know it will get plenty of headlines, provoke a response from the public, and thus get publicity for their podcast, TV show, whatever.

For my part, obviously I'm aware that the microphone is there when I'm refereeing matches. Let's say I'm conscious of it, but it can't have any bearing on how I do the game and I most certainly don't make decisions, or say things, to court publicity, or for it to go viral. In fact, something I'm not comfortable with when watching matches today is the buzzword amongst referees, which is 'selling' their decisions. Even if you're wrong in brandishing a red card, or indeed choosing not to give one, everybody thinks you're right because you're using the microphone to 'sell' it. Some referees' managers even say in the review process that they can understand the decision because, 'You explained it well.'

I don't agree with that at all. I say to referees, 'Look, just make the right decision in the first place and explain why. If you do that, you don't need to "sell" it, the decision sells itself.' For me, it doesn't matter how well you explain a decision on the mic, if it's wrong it's wrong and you need to learn from it. I certainly made enough errors myself, but crucially I always tried to learn from them for the next time. It's important that you don't referee to an audience, you simply referee the players on the pitch. Don't try to be somebody you're not.

Ironic advice, you might think, given how so many of my own remarks did the rounds on social media, but that's the point: it's just me being me, calling a situation exactly as I see it at the time. I certainly don't do it thinking, Oh, if I say this it'll go viral. Yes that's happened, sometimes it's worked to my advantage, I guess, sometimes it certainly hasn't – and I even end up looking a little bit silly.

Like the time when I shouted 'Everybody in', calling the 30 players together during a really bad-tempered clash between Scarlets and Leinster to tell them I'd had enough of a whole series of off-the-ball incidents and that it had to stop. Now I wasn't even supposed to be doing that game, the Irish official Alain Rolland was down for it and I was meant to be refereeing a match in Ireland. But the weather was freezing cold, there were concerns about flight delays and travelling, so it was decided two days in advance that we'd switch fixtures – Alain would stay in Ireland and take charge of my intended game and I'd remain in Wales for his.

Thanks Alain! It was a nasty affair, lots of stuff going on, much of it behind my back. Seán O'Brien, a real hard man but a wonderful player, was getting stuck-in for Leinster; a few Scarlets, in particular their scrum-half Tavis Knoyle, one of the great characters of the game, were doing likewise in return. It was starting to get towards breaking point when a late tackle by O'Brien, that neither I nor my assistants had seen, sparked a brawl 30 yards away from where I was standing, having just awarded the Scarlets a penalty for offside.

I looked across at what was happening with the two sets of players and decided I'd had enough. I blew my whistle, motioned with my hand and shouted, 'Everybody in please. Get everybody in here.' Just to make sure there was no doubt among the players, I repeated 'Get everybody in here' two more times. It was a while before all 30 players gathered around me. They were probably a little bit shocked by the demand – indeed the great Brian O'Driscoll's face at that moment was a picture, and will always stay with me – but when they did, it was time to lay down the law.

'Things like this are not acceptable in the game. What happened here and what happened afterwards I did not see. It ends there, is that clear? You're adults, you'll be treated like it as long as you behave like it.'

Of course, the legendary Welsh fly-half and dual-code ace turned top pundit Jonathan Davies, a great friend of mine who was doing the TV commentary with the wonderful Gareth Charles, immediately picked up on my fatal mistake. 'He's not going to make an issue of it … yet he calls all 30 players in!' Jiffy informed the viewers. Fair enough, he'd got me there, although I suppose at least that was a bit of a humorous ending to something that had got badly out of hand on the field.

Immediately after the dressing-down, one of my touch judges, Colin Kirkhouse, said through the comms into my earpiece, 'Great, nothing better than a good bust-up to get the crowd going!' Usually, at Parc y Scarlets, just seeing my name down as referee in the match-day programme is enough to get them going, mind!

It's not often you actually have to speak to 30 players. One or two, perhaps, like in the Harlequins versus Wasps European Champions Cup game at the Stoop in January 2015, when I noticed rival locks George Robson and Bradley Davies grappling off the ball. A bit of pushing and shoving, huffing and puffing. I was almost thinking, if you're going to throw a punch, damn well throw one!

As referee I had to intervene. 'OK, that's enough, leave it,' I told them both. Still they continued, so I spoke again. 'It's embarrassing, will you leave it and get on with it please – if you want to *cwtch*, do it off the field, not on it!'

Fortunately the two of them stopped and we were able to get on with the game, my sole intention. Once more I didn't think too much of it, but BT Sport tweeted out the moment with the caption, 'Ref Nigel Owens puts George Robson and Bradley Davies in their place with a classic one-liner.' Cue another one going viral. Bradley, capped 66 times by Wales, just smiled at my remark. George, from Stourbridge in the Midlands, told me afterwards, 'I didn't know what *cwtch* meant, I had to ask!' For others who don't, it's a Welsh word for cuddle, or hug.

There was another England–Wales one when I finally

got the opportunity to referee the Oxford versus Cambridge Varsity match at Twickenham. This was a fixture I'd wanted to do for a number of years but which unfortunately always seemed to clash with a European Cup game a couple of days later, and the powers-that-be didn't want me to risk injury. I got my wish in 2018 and when there was a break in play, with one of the Cambridge players needing treatment, I asked one of his team-mates if I could have a swig of his drink, and in doing so applauded him on the tremendous commitment being put in.

'Thank you sir,' he replied.

'No need to call me sir – I'm from west Wales,' I said.

A bit trivial, really, but yet again it was put on to the internet and had a ridiculous number of shares. In England they often call the referee 'sir'. It doesn't happen so much in Wales, nor do I particularly like it either. I'd much rather be called 'Ref' or 'Nigel'.

There was a funny upshot to this one too, which didn't appear on the internet. Another Cambridge player approached me to say, 'I'm from west Wales as well, Nigel – and I've been telling them not to call me sir, too!'

We both laughed. Humour is a really good thing and has been a part of me since I was doing stand-up on stage as a teenager. So when a ball boy threw a ball back in at a Leinster versus Scarlets game and it accidentally hit me on the back of my head, I reacted in the only way I could. Out came the yellow card – the crowd, who had roared when the ball first struck me, laughed again. I didn't see it as playing to the audience, it was a bit of fun. Surely, even as a referee you can be normal. Maybe that's why these clips do go viral; people like to see someone in the public eye, so to speak, just being his natural and chatty self. I posted my jersey to the ball boy after the game. He was made-up.

I had to give away another jersey after an encounter in Dublin when I was called in at the last minute to run touch for Ireland versus Argentina, as the assistant referee went down with food poisoning. I was already in the country, having done a game in Connacht on the Friday night. So a quick change of travel plans and instead of coming home to Wales, off I went to the Aviva Stadium. Whilst warming up and doing a bit of calf stretching on the advertising boards, a group of 12 young Irish supporters from Ulster, aged between 15 and 16, were shouting 'Hey Nige, quick selfie' and trying to get me into a photo. I cheekily stuck up two fingers and smiled. They thought it was hilarious, and cheered me throughout the first half while I was on their side of the pitch.

Guess what? The photo they posted on social media went viral. Thankfully, most saw it in the humour I'd intended, although inevitably the odd one or two deemed that what I'd done was unacceptable. Get a sense of humour was my response – and that of the lads, too. I sent my jersey to the young lad Gareth Duncan, who had the phone. A few months later, when I was in Ulster refereeing a game, he and his parents came to meet me at the ground and gave me a little present in return. It really made my day.

Of course, social media does not see that kind of thing. But another one that did the rounds, in Ireland once more, came at a Munster versus Glasgow game in Musgrave Park back in 2012, at a time when there were still a few communication issues being ironed out between referees and TMOs. In the event of a problem back then, we had a system whereby the TMO would contact the number four official by mobile phone and tell him to let me know whether a try could be awarded or not. The number four is the man on the side of the pitch doing replacements and other administrative duties, so he was ideally placed to give me a signal.

Just my luck, that day the communications did break down as I questioned whether a try by the Munster wing Felix Jones could be given. I waited for the yes or no signal from the side of the pitch – only this time, instead of communicating himself as he was supposed to, the number four actually ran onto the pitch and handed the phone to me so that I could speak directly to the TMO. So I'm standing out there in the middle, mobile to my left ear, finger in my right ear so I could blot out the crowd noise, trying to hear what he was saying and deal with it myself in this rather cumbersome manner. Some people were even questioning whether I was speaking on the phone to someone back home in Wales while awaiting the TMO's decision! Some you just can't win I guess, but that's the true story behind Nigel Owens and that mobile incident.

Two more clips that went viral actually came from the same match, Tonga versus Georgia in a Pool C clash played at Gloucester's wonderfully historic Kingsholm ground during the 2015 World Cup. As I awarded a penalty to Georgia, their captain Mamuka Gorgodze said to me, 'I'll take the three points, Nige.'

'I can't give you the three points, but I will give you a go!' I responded with a hint of a smile.

I watch referees today and sometimes they don't seem to be enjoying games, which in turn affects their performances. I loved being out there in the middle. I was at the height of my powers and, I guess, that came across with some of the comments that came so naturally to me. But they weren't that funny to justify going viral, mind. Gorgodze, a lovely gentle giant of a guy, burst into a big grin and told his full-back and kicker Merab Kvirikashvili to go for goal – which he successfully did. So Georgia got their three points in the end, en route to a 17–10 victory.

Earlier in the game there had been another seemingly completely innocuous moment to me, this time involving Georgia's prop Davit Zirakashvili, a strong scrummager but who, like all the best front-row forwards, certainly knew the dark arts of scrum time. I felt he was engaging a little too early and explained there needed to be a space between my calls of bind and set. He seemed to suggest I was speaking a little too quickly and didn't understand me.

'How many times have I refereed you? And you don't understand me still?' I queried. 'I'll shout louder then, OK?'

Zirakashvili had played for Clermont in France for ten years. This was his third World Cup, and we both knew what was going on here really. As I spoke he held up both hands and broke into a smile and was as good as gold for the rest of the game. Message received again.

The TV match commentator chipped in with, 'I think Nigel's saying "Don't use that language barrier excuse with me, sunshine",' his reaction doubtless one of the reasons why the clip became so popular.

Any referee in the world will tell you that the scrums can be an absolute nightmare to officiate. You are looking out for so much and canny old warhorses like Zirakashvili certainly keep you on your toes. But by this stage of my career I was well accustomed to dealing with such issues, thanks to some excellent advice I was given early on by one of my great mentors, Derek Bevan.

I owe so much to Bev. He was my coach for many years, my friend, my confidante, a pillar of strength – and just a great guy to be around. He'd been a truly great referee in his own right, officiating at the highest level between 1984 to 2000 and taking charge of the 1991 World Cup final between England and Australia at Twickenham. Bev was born just 16 miles down the road from me in west Wales. At the time of writing this book, there have only been nine Rugby World Cup finals. Extraordinary to think, then, that two of them have been refereed by officials from this particular part of the world. Must be something in the water down here!

Bev was right by my side to offer his words of wisdom as TMO in my first major European Cup game, Bristol versus Leinster at the Memorial Ground in 2003. It was the final group game and the presumption was that nothing would be riding on this particular fixture, the kind of match inexperienced officials, as I was back then, were appointed to in order to cut their teeth at that level. However, Bristol had pulled off a seismic shock the week before by beating Montferrand out in France, a result no-one expected, and it suddenly meant there was a lot at stake, plenty of needle and a far more competitive affair than the organisers had envisaged.

There was something of a comical start to the day after I picked up Bev and Clayton Thomas, my touch judge. We parked at the ground, only to almost immediately see another car pull up two spaces away with the number plate B1G REF. It was Clive Norling, who else – like Bev another truly great Welsh referee in his own right, who was now the

WRU's referees' manager. Clive had just sent out a letter to all of us saying that it had come to his attention that petrol expenses were being put in when he believed officials were, in actual fact, sharing car journeys. If so, this practice had to cease at once, he stressed.

So here Clive was – two spaces away from us. Bev opens the back door and tries to crawl out without being seen. Clayton crouches down in the front and attempts to hide. Unfortunately for them both, the big man didn't miss too much when he was refereeing and he certainly spotted this one.

'How are you all?' said Clive in that unique big booming voice of his. 'I'm looking forward to seeing just one expense sheet on Monday morning.'

Of course, Bev and Clayton then started having a go at me. Why did I have to park there, why couldn't I have gone further along the car park where he wouldn't have spotted us? As if it was all my fault!

As for the game itself, considering what was at stake it went reasonably well, other than the scrums. They were a complete and utter mess. I kept having to speak to the two front rows, but it proved to no avail. I was young and inexperienced, it was my first game at this level, and they were taking advantage.

This is when Derek stepped in with his advice after the game. 'Listen Nigel, the front-row players don't care one jot about you – so you shouldn't care one jot about them, either,' he started. 'The next time you referee a game and have to call them out, you tell them this. "Look, I've asked you once, now I'm damn well TELLING you – keep that scrum up, otherwise you're going off." And make sure they know you mean it, too. Don't let them dictate to you – you're the man in charge, you put them in their place.'

I've never forgotten those words and have used them a few times. They certainly did help me in getting good control and results in the scrum, and to deal so comfortably in my own way with Zirakashvili 12 years later at the World Cup, and for many other scrum misdemeanours, too. Like the time Cardiff Blues were playing the Ospreys in front of a bumper crowd, two star-studded teams at the time, full of their Galáctico players. It was a great atmosphere, a super game, but the scrum was a real problem. Gethin Jenkins, the Blues loosehead, and Adam Jones, his direct opponent, had been part of the Lions Test front row against world champions South Africa in 2009, and I'd had enough.

'I thought you two were supposed to be the best props in the world – well it's about time you started to behave like it. Keep the scrums up please.' To be fair, they got better after that, as you'd expect from two such wonderful front rowers as Gethin and Adam, who didn't win 234 Test caps between them for no reason.

There was another Cardiff Blues game, this time against the Scarlets, when the scrums were fine – until a couple of replacement props came on and the scrums now turned into a complete mess. I explained we'd had no issues up to that point in the game, so clearly it wasn't my problem, nor that of the two players they'd just replaced, so it had to be solely down to them. 'If this is the way you scrummage, no wonder you're not starting the game!' I told them, in a semi-humorous tone, making it clear they couldn't just come on and spoil the game for everyone else. They were both smiling, took my comment in the spirit in which it was meant, and made sure the scrums stayed up after that.

Same in a Heineken Cup knockout match between Munster and Toulouse at Thomond Park when the scrums were a mess again and I had to address both front rows.

'You don't like to scrummage? Well if you don't, you're in the wrong position. The next one to cause problems, you're going off for ten minutes. You've all been at fault and you've all had your final warnings. Is that clear? Get on with it please.'

The TV commentator said, 'I wish there was a quotes book for Nigel Owens', and once more it went viral, but Bev would certainly have approved of the way I took on board that early lesson and acted upon it. Bev was so much more than my mentor and coach, mind. We had an absolute scream, he was such great company to be around, although I'm not sure I was smiling too much when he was my TMO in a European Cup game out in France. Not at the time anyway, although I can smile about it now. We had a code word of 'trigger', which Derek would shout in my ear if I'd missed something blatantly obvious out on the pitch. So if I and my two assistant referees weren't quite sure about a forward pass, or a knock-on, we would let the action continue briefly and Bev would then very quickly come in with 'trigger, trigger, trigger', which meant I could go back to my original hunch without having to ask officially. His words were my trigger to act. It was a great system, albeit a little out of protocol as, back then, the TMO was only allowed to comment about the grounding of a try or foul play, unlike today when they come in for pretty much everything. Far too much I'd say, but that's another conversation for another day.

Just before kick-off in this particular game out in France, Bev said, 'Nigel, same again, if it's blatant to all the world, but you haven't seen it, I'll come in with trigger.' Twenty-five minutes into the action, I thought I'd spotted something, wasn't completely sure, let play go on and Bev suddenly shouts, 'Del Boy, Del Boy' in my ear. I stopped in my tracks, wondering what on earth he meant? As I wasn't sure, I let play carry on.

At half-time, when Bev came down from the truck, I asked him, 'What the b****y heck is Del Boy?'

He said they'd just announced on the news that Roger Lloyd-Pack, the actor who played the brilliantly funny character Trigger from *Only Fools and Horses*, had sadly passed away. 'So I couldn't say "trigger" in case people were listening in and got the wrong idea,' Derek said.

'B****y Del Boy! How am I supposed to know what you meant by Del Boy?' I asked.

'Well it's the same f*****g programme, you must have known!' was Bev's response.

We were all in fits of laughter in the changing room. Priceless. Imagine if that one had been caught on the mic!

One that was, and once more did the rounds on the internet, came when I was doing Ospreys versus Cardiff Blues in 2014. I thought a try had been scored, wanted to double-check the grounding was OK, so asked, 'Derek, any reason why I can't award the try?'

He took a quick look on the TMO monitor, then replied, 'Nige, there is no reason I can't give you that you cannot award the try!'

First Del Boy, now what on earth did this gobbledygook mean? I had to de-code and semi-repeat Bev's words back to him, asking at the end, 'That means I can award the try?'

'That is it,' replied Derek. We got there in the end.

Derek actually wasn't big on being TMO but, of the

300-odd times he did the job, the vast majority were with me, to offer his help – and, I should stress, to have a good night out because a few pints after a game were an absolute prerequisite for Bev. Provided, of course, the match had gone well and it was OK to be seen in public. Otherwise we'd stay in the hotel.

Crikey we had some laughs, even after a bruising Heineken Cup showdown at Ravenhill shortly before Christmas in 2012 when Ulster surprisingly lost 9–10 at home to Northampton. It was a tough, niggly game, the Ulster crowd were booing me loudly, and I walked back to the changing rooms afterwards mentally and physically exhausted.

As Bev came down from his TMO truck his first words were, 'Well done Nige, you've just spoilt a good night out.'

As it happens, we did venture out onto the streets of Belfast and ended up in an ex-navy and -servicemen's club where there was an old guy in his sixties playing music. By the end of the night I was on stage with him myself, singing along. Last orders were called and a woman, well into her seventies, bolted to the bar and ordered three Baileys and ice, half a lager, and same again for her friend! She was certainly having a good time and got chatting to Bev.

Earlier in the day we had visited the *Titanic* centre in Belfast, where the iconic ship was built of course, and this woman asked Bev if anything big had been made in Wales. Straight away he replied *Moby Dick*, the famous 1950s film about a whale starring Gregory Peck, which was partly shot in the west Wales coastal town of Fishguard.

'Yeah, there's a few moby dicks around here too,' replied this elderly woman quick as a flash. We were in hysterics.

As we were on another occasion in Ulster, when Bev was

speaking to the taxi driver transporting us to our hotel. He was telling us of places to visit and the history of the city and was clearly incredibly proud that the *Titanic* had been built in the city's Harland & Wolff shipyard.

Bev couldn't resist. 'Yes I heard,' he said. 'Didn't it sink?'

There was a hushed silence in the car. We didn't know how the taxi driver would respond, whether he'd even throw us out. After a pause, he replied, 'There was f**k-all wrong with it when it left here, let me tell you.' He was not overly pleased with Bev for saying what he did, but it was typical of the kind of fun we had together. Derek is such a great laugh, completely inoffensive and means no harm. If more were like him, particularly on social media which can sometimes prove to be such a hostile environment, then the world would be a much better place, let me tell you that.

Social media. Where do I begin? It can be bad, it can be very good. I've seen both sides. I've never been a whiz kid on computers. I can use email and that's about it – and that's how it's going to stay, too. But I first became aware of Twitter and Facebook during the 2007 World Cup when one of my colleagues, the South African referee Jonathan Kaplan, was using it and I began to realise it could be very useful. Given I have in excess of 425,000 Twitter followers, it means that I can use the platform to promote the charities of which I'm an ambassador, speak out against injustices, even explain refereeing decisions at times when some don't fully understand why a particular call was made.

I also notice the good that social media can do for people going through bad times, such as with mental health issues, eating disorders, anxiety, struggles of pressure at work, and how others sharing their experiences on such a public network can help those in trouble.

When football's European Super League was so controversially put forward in the spring of 2021, social media played a huge role. It galvanised supporters, players and pundits to successfully campaign against the ghastly concept an elite group of clubs tried to bring in because of greed, selfishness and their attempt to have greater power. The public fought it together as a common cause, proving a bandwagon can roll.

These are massive plusses to social media, and I've seen the benefits personally too, I guess. There were lots of comments about 'Nigel Owens being the best ref in the world', or 'Nigel Owens must get the World Cup final', which received plenty of likes and shares. And I suppose the various aforementioned clips with players that have gone viral increased my popularity not only amongst the rugby public, but beyond that as well. So it would be stupid to suggest I'm not aware of the huge positives social media can bring. I do and fully appreciate it.

Sadly, I've also seen the uglier side as well, when keyboard warriors cross the line, are abusive and indeed at times have almost victimised me for my sexuality, using horrible homophobic comments and bad language against me. Lots of people in the public eye get this and it can hurt. No matter how high your profile, you are still just a human being; you have a mum and dad, are someone's husband, wife, partner. It's not necessarily the person being targeted who is hurt the most, it's those loved ones around them who feel it and take it badly. Imagine the children seeing such vile, nasty comments of hate or threats made against their mum or dad just because they happen to be famous.

I really have no problem with people whose beliefs completely differ to mine and who put those views forward politely in the public domain. Someone told me that he didn't feel that gay people should be able to marry or have children; he didn't have any issue whatsoever with my sexuality, just felt a traditional husband and wife was different to a gay couple and that's what marriage really meant in his eyes. I didn't agree, but I understood his viewpoint and we were able to have a civilised discussion about it. Some people express a wish for a return of the death sentence for the most heinous of crimes. That doesn't make you a horrible person, it's their honestly held belief and social media offers a platform where they can express those views and they shouldn't just be howled down for them.

The key here though is being polite, respectful to everyone's personal opinion and not crossing the line with hateful or vindictive words. Unfortunately, hate is too prevalent and when idiots do overstep the mark, often hiding behind anonymity, they should be held accountable for their actions. Free speech is important – we must never ever lose that – but what isn't acceptable is spreading hate and breaking the law. The social media platforms need more robust checks in place and, anonymity or not, they have to find a way of banning the offending individuals from their platforms.

I've had lots of people question me on social media after matches, even saying Nigel Owens looked particularly grumpy that day, and did he get out of bed the wrong side? Sometimes it's made me think they've got a point and I will lighten up a little. If I feel I've got a decision wrong, I'll hold up my hands. Fair enough.

On other occasions, when there's been unnecessary abuse, I will respond by having a go back. France versus

England in the 2020 Six Nations, when Eddie Jones' side were on the wrong end of a 24–17 opening day Le Crunch defeat in Paris; surprise, surprise, it was all the fault of yours truly as the referee.

One supporter called me a 'w***er' on Twitter. Instead of letting it go, I simply responded: 'It's a shame your father wasn't one.' *Wales Online* picked up on what I'd said and reported, 'Rugby fans across the world loved Nigel Owens' reply to a Twitter troll, with thousands liking it within minutes.' But I didn't say it to get that kind of response, it was simply the first thing that came into my head.

I'd previously heard the comment whilst refereeing a Scarlets versus Cardiff game at Stradey Park many years earlier when the home crowd, who can be quite one-eyed down there at times, were booing me after I'd awarded a penalty against their team. As I headed towards the tunnel at half-time I heard a Scarlets supporter shout, 'Nigel, you're a w***er,' before his mate responded, 'Pity his father wasn't.' I thought it quite funny at the time, smiled inwardly and have used the line in after-dinner speeches, so it just came naturally when this Twitter abuser had tagged me into his post.

There was another England fan who called me a four-letter word. I noticed he had about 400,000 Twitter followers, which is a large number, so again, rather than just ignore it, I responded: 'What a wonderful example to people on Twitter with language like that. I have no idea who you are, or what you do, but with so many followers surely you should show a bit of a better example to them. Have a good day. X.'

A lot of people seemed to latch on to that one too, saying, 'Well done, Nige.'

Listen, people can criticise my refereeing, I know that goes with the territory. I'm human, and like everyone else I make mistakes, but there is no need in society for blatant rudeness and name-calling. People tell me I'm better off just ignoring this abuse, but I disagree with that at times. There is a responsibility in how you say things on social media, but as I've pointed out previously perhaps there is also a responsibility sometimes not to just stand by and say nothing when someone has badly overstepped the mark. Some people, of course, are just plain horrible and there can be no reasoning with them, but occasionally you need to stand up to these individuals. Often, when you do, they will back off and realise the error of their ways.

What the England fans criticising me that day didn't know was the beautiful gesture given to me by Red Rose skipper Owen Farrell and the rest of Eddie Jones' team. It was a pulsating encounter, the Stade de France was as loud as I've ever known it, so much so that some of the forwards were asking me to shout louder on the scrum set-up calls because they couldn't hear me. 'I will try,' I told them, 'But there are 80,000 people shouting louder than me!'

At the end the England players were very complimentary towards me, I even had a hug off Farrell. A few others, Kyle Sinckler, Ben Youngs and Ellis Genge amongst them, came up to say thank you for refereeing the game. Perhaps they sensed it might prove to be my final Six Nations match and wished to show their appreciation. One or two fans may have been critical of me on social media, but the England players could not have been more courteous, as Farrell presented me with one of their white jerseys which read: 'France v England, Six Nations, Le Crunch, Nigel Owens 98th Test.'

On the back of the jersey it just had a big '98'. It was such a touching gesture. I'm aware that some people out there seem to think England are arrogant. I know Welsh fans love to hate them – although, it must be stressed, that's very much in terms of traditional rugby rivalry only. But I've obviously got to know the England squad and management quite well over the years and I can tell you that they are amongst the most down-to-earth, decent people you could ever wish to meet.

Even in defeat in Paris, England behaved with incredible dignity towards me and I wasn't going to let a few abusers on social media spoil that.

There was a more high-profile Twitter spat, shall we call it, between myself and *I'm A Celebrity* star Nick Knowles after another England loss, this time to Scotland in the only Calcutta Cup match I refereed between the two teams. The Six Nations game at Murrayfield, in February 2018, was won 25–13 by the Scots, their first victory over the English in a decade.

If truth be told, the Scots fully deserved their triumph, with Huw Jones (two) and Sean Maitland scoring the tries as they raced into an unassailable 22–6 lead, but clearly Nick disagreed A passionate and avid England fan, he questioned some of my decision-making, posting on Twitter: 'So @nigelrefowens singlehandedly trying to avenge the England defeat of Wales – let them play. Refs are not the stars of the show.'

That was a reference to England having beaten Warren Gatland's Wales 12–6 at Twickenham a couple of weeks earlier. As if that would have any bearing whatsoever upon my decision-making. Again, by all means criticise my refereeing calls, but please don't accuse me of bias.

Instead of ignoring Nick, I went public in saying just that in response to his tweet. Once more lots of people supported me, tagging Nick into so many that he ended up tweeting: 'It's hilarious how if you criticise Nigel Owens the whole of Wales gets on your back. He's not Llywelyn ap Gruffudd.'

One of Nick's concerns was that I called back Danny Care after he stole the ball off a Scottish player and was about to score a try, awarding Scotland a penalty instead because Joe Launchbury had gone off his feet at a ruck in the first place. I should have blown the whistle there and then, but I didn't expect Care to nick the ball and thought Scotland would have an advantage, thus played on for a while. My decision to call back Care was 100 per cent correct; what I wished I'd done was award the penalty against Launchbury two or three seconds earlier, which meant Nick would never have had his ammunition in the first place. But try explaining all that within the limited characters Twitter offers you!

I had a bit of fun afterwards, dressing up as a builder for the S4C TV chat show hosted by Jonathan Davies and challenging Nick, 'I'm going to have a job share. I'll have a go at building, and he will have a go at being a referee. And then we'll see how good he is.' I blocked him. He can call me anything he wants, but don't call me a cheat.

Anyway, we pretty quickly buried the hatchet. Nick posted a picture of the two of us smiling together at Twickenham the following year, after England had thrashed France 44–8, with the words: 'OK, you can call off the Welsh Fatwah, we've made up. I can visit Welsh family again.'

Nick caused me a bit of grief at the time, but I wasn't going to hold it against him. Crikey, if I held a grudge and refused to speak to people who say something bad about my refereeing, I probably wouldn't be speaking to anybody at all!

CHAPTER FOUR

How it all began (or very nearly didn't)

MY REFEREEING CAREER could actually have finished pretty much before it even started.

Why? Because in only my third game in the middle, and second senior match, one of the teams walked off the pitch in protest at my handling of the game. Not just any team I might add: this was Dyfed-Powys Police, albeit their B side, grown men in huge positions of responsibility which a 16-year-old impressionable youngster, as I was at the time, had been taught to look up to in life.

They were in the Llanelli and District League back then and, led by their captain, they refused to play on because they felt I was refereeing unfairly and giving an advantage to their opponents Cefneithin, the village just down the road from my home. Yet I have never ever, and I do mean never, favoured one team over another. Not then, not since, not in the future. I'm always totally neutral. As I was told by the great former Welsh referee Clive Norling when I started out, 'You are going to have bad days on the field, just as in life – but as long as you are bad to both sides, then don't worry about it, learn, improve and move on.'

Towards the end of my career I was even afforded the incredible opportunity to referee my own country Wales in an international match, against the Barbarians, at the Principality Stadium. There was a huge crowd inside the iconic Cardiff ground that day, fervent Welsh men and women keen to see their team win – and doubtless hoping a referee from Wales would play ball a teeny bit! Not a chance. There is no prouder Welshman on this planet than yours truly, but to me that day it was simply a case of red versus black. As a referee, it's in your DNA to treat the two teams exactly the same, fairly and with respect, whatever the circumstances or occasion.

Do you know, one of the greatest compliments paid to me is from England fans saying they wish I could have refereed their Six Nations matches against Wales. That intense rivalry goes back decades and matches New Zealand versus South Africa as the biggest in rugby, yet I often heard the comment from England supporters, normally after I'd just taken charge of one of their games at Twickenham.

'We just know you'd do it fairly Nigel,' they'd say. I genuinely think I would have, too, red versus white, with national loyalties put aside for 80 minutes, not that the situation ever arose, of course. Mind, had it done and England won as a result of one of my decisions, I'd probably never have been able to set foot on the Welsh side of the Severn Bridge again! Such are the passions, emotions and feelings that go with rugby.

It can get very tribal, every team wants to win badly, whatever the level. Nothing, however, could justify the actions of the Dyfed-Powys Police team that day, which really hurt me. It was my first bad experience as a referee, scared me in one sense, certainly disappointed me. I'm not having this, I thought to myself. If this is the kind of rubbish I have to deal with I'd rather give up refereeing, even though I had only just taken up the whistle. For a while it really was touch-and-go, my decision could have gone either way. I spoke to friends about my concerns, while my headmaster at school also got to hear about it.

That was when a lovely old guy called Onfil Pickard, a big noise in refereeing circles in west Wales, stepped in to offer some worldly words of advice that held me in good stead not only during those early days, but indeed for the entirety of my career. He came down to the school to see me and said, 'Let me tell you something very important, young Nigel. As a referee you will get good reviews, but there will also always be an element of criticism and even rudeness, it goes with the territory. You mustn't let it get to you. Never.'

He explained that my decisions would be correct the majority of the time, how some constructive criticism is justified in terms of how I can improve, but downright abuse is never acceptable. Nor was what the Police players did that afternoon, Onfil stressing they would be dealt with via the disciplinary process.

'But whatever you do, don't let them force you into finishing,' he urged.

I've never forgotten those kindly words and I decided, no, I wasn't packing it in after just a handful of matches. I'd started to enjoy being a referee too much for that. Onfil's words stayed with me throughout the rest of my career. How true they proved to be.

I've read many nice comments about my refereeing on social media or in the press, but there are plenty that aren't particularly complimentary, too. I learned to take the good with the bad – but the better you are, the more the good outweighs the bad.

My move into refereeing in the first place actually began, believe it or not, with a failed conversion kick as a school player just a few months earlier. From right in front of the posts too – although, in hindsight, given everything that I managed to achieve subsequently, I guess it kind of proved to be the best thing to happen to me.

Rewind even further back momentarily, though. It was at the age of around five or six that I first became interested in rugby, having watched an old Five Nations match on television in 1977 when the late and truly great Wales fly-half Phil Bennett scored a memorable length-of-field try against Scotland up at Murrayfield. The ball passed through several Welsh hands before Bennett, involved in the move early on, rounded it off with a dazzling side-step to score by the posts. The BBC commentator Bill McLaren, himself a proud Scot, was clearly spellbound as he uttered the words, 'Oh this is going to be the try of the Championship,' when Bennett raced in, followed by, 'That was absolute magic – and the whole crowd here knows it.'

It certainly made its mark on me. I went straight out onto the field behind my council house home in the little Welsh village of Mynyddcerrig, where I was born in 1971 and raised, rugby ball in hand, pretending to be Phil Bennett and darting in and out of a couple of donkeys who I decided were Scottish defenders. Chocolate and Fudge were their names. They were probably a little bewildered as I raced in between them over and over again to replicate Benny's try.

Mynyddcerrig is a lovely little place, lying a shade over 60 miles north-west of Cardiff. It has a small population, everyone knows everyone else, therefore many from the village itself and the surrounding areas are friends and family. I owe everything to the upbringing I was given by my mum Mair and my dad Geraint, who followed my refereeing career closely and were incredibly supportive.

We didn't have junior rugby clubs on a Sunday morning back then. As such, a handful of us tended to kick a football around on the yard of Mynyddcerrig Primary School, which sadly was to close in 2007. There were only around 15 or 16 in the whole school, so we'd play one in goal, a few out, and last one to score would swap places with the goalkeeper. Then we'd go around again, and so on.

I didn't even start speaking English until I was about six years of age and they began teaching it in school. We'd only talk in Welsh at home and it was only when a few non-Welsh-speaking families moved into the village, with kids the same age as me who became friends, that things began to change.

I guess the rugby started properly in my final year of primary school, when I tried my hand as a Number 8. Then I had a go at prop forward on moving up to the nearby Gwendraeth Grammar School – which was phased out and became a comprehensive in 1983 – before moving to full-back after switching to my new Welsh-speaking school of Maes-yr-Yrfa.

At first many parents thought Gwendraeth would remain a grammar school, so a lot of pupils stayed there and it meant that the numbers at Maes-yr-Yrfa were pretty low. As such, we often struggled to put a rugby team on the field and we tended to get beaten. Before the game that changed everything for me – away to Ysgol Griffith Jones from nearby St Clears, when I was 16 and in fifth form, or

Year 11 as it is known today – we hadn't won a single match all season, and were beaten by 60 points by Gwendraeth. So when we travelled west by bus, Year 7 and Year 8 also in tow for fixtures of their own, there wasn't much expectation of that losing streak coming to an end.

Well, wonders will never cease. One of my best mates, Wayne Thomas, a really decent centre who went on to play for Bonymaen in Welsh Division One, demonstrated his class by scoring a wonderful try right under the posts in the final minute to make it 12–12. We had a match-winning conversion to come, literally the last kick of the game, and I went straight up to captain Craig Bonnell, another of my big mates, to say I'd take it. I could see my name up in lights, the hero of the school with the winning kick. Heck, they'd probably even chair me off the pitch in celebration.

To add to the sense of drama, the Year 7 and Year 8 games had finished five minutes earlier and they were all gathered around the pitch to watch the big moment, creating quite a bit of an atmosphere for a school match. That kick really couldn't have been any easier, or closer. Up I stepped to supposedly make it 12–14, our first win of the season – but the ball sliced closer to the damn corner flag than the posts! A few of the St Clears pupils, scarcely able to believe what they'd just seen, started cheering – and laughing – at my mishap and their great fortune in escaping with a draw. The reaction of my mates was the exact opposite. They were fuming. You useless so-and-so, what the heck were you doing?

Then it was the turn of John Beynon, our games master, to have his say. John was a great guy. A lot of after-school activities had been cut following the teachers' strike but he was always around in his own time to help and encourage pupils with rugby. I was out in South Africa refereeing the World Rugby Sevens when I learned that John had passed away. I couldn't make the funeral, so myself and Gareth 'Babs' Williams, the ex-Wales forwards' coach who then joined the Scarlets backroom staff and was captain of the Welsh Sevens squad for many years, paid our respects before one of the games with a moment's silence together to remember him. I didn't let play start in my game until I'd done that. I owed so much to him.

Anyway, back to my missed conversion. Clearly unhappy, John came up to me to say in Welsh, '*Nigel, shwt uffern missos ti hwnna, odd e o flaen y blydi post 'achan. Pam na ei di i ddyfarnu, neu rhwbeth arall, yn lle?*' Translated into English, 'Nigel, how the heck can you miss that, it was right in front of the posts mun. Why don't you go and referee or something, instead?'

Then he turned his ire onto poor Craig Bonnell, my big mate. 'What on earth were you doing letting him take such an important conversion? You know what his kicking is like.' Craig was sheepish. As for myself, I guess those immortal words of advice from John changed everything. I did indeed try my hand at refereeing.

Completely coincidentally, the following week our old woodwork teacher James Rees brought some posters into school about a Welsh Rugby Union campaign to recruit referees. The poster had a picture of First World War hero Field Marshal Horatio Herbert Kitchener pointing a finger, with the words, 'Your country needs you', and given it was common knowledge by now what John Beynon had said to me, I went to see him and he suggested I initially help with some inter-house games.

That was my first taste of refereeing, and at the age of

16 I kind of had the bug. I joined the Llanelli and District Referees' Society, eventually becoming its chairman – a position I still proudly hold today after 25 years, and where we have meetings on the last Thursday of every month. However, this year will be my last term as chairman though. It's time to hand over the baton to someone else after a quarter of a century, although I will always be a part of the society and its members, who I owe a lot to.

Like two influential older gentlemen who were on the committee back then and who came down to run the rule over me in school matches, the aforementioned Onfil Pickard and Alun West, who was fixtures' secretary and thus organised which matches you were given. Alun passed away recently at the age of 85, but I will never forget the debt I owe him. Such a lovely guy, he was one of the main reasons I started refereeing in the first place.

Alun and Onfil evidently decided early on that I'd done well enough in those inter-house matches because I was quickly handed my first game on my own, so to speak, a Welsh Schools Dewar Shield match between Carmarthenshire Schools and nearby rivals Pembrokeshire Schools. It was played at a venue called Five Fields, and when people ask me where I started refereeing, I always tell them the same thing – somewhere in between the bread and milk counter and the fruit and veg counter at Tesco's in Carmarthen. They built a big superstore on the site around 13 years ago, you see.

This game was clearly a huge test for me so I was delighted afterwards when Alun said, 'You know what Nigel, that was a good game … a damn good game,' before giving me a few pointers of things to work on. Onfil also told me I'd done well, but perhaps even more pleasing were the words of a complete stranger. An old guy, a grandparent of one of the kids, knocked on the changing room door and asked if he could come in.

'They tell me this was your first game as a referee?'

'Yes,' I replied.

'Well done,' he said kindly. 'Well done. You carry on like that and you'll have a good future in refereeing.'

I was on cloud nine as I walked back to the car where my dad was waiting. He too agreed that I'd done well, and things started to happen very quickly because Alun said I could start refereeing seniors rugby and second XV matches to get into the swing of it all. Wow, this was a quick elevation. My only request to Alun was to keep any games reasonably local because, obviously, I couldn't drive at 16, while my dad struggled with roundabouts and dual carriageways so wasn't happy doing distances.

On one occasion when dad was visiting mum in hospital, he took the back roads – until there were no more, just a roundabout and dual carriageway for the final part of the journey. As he approached the roundabout, instead of driving to the left around it he took an immediate right turn. Luckily, a kind passing motorist spotted what happened, pulled his car across to stop the traffic, turned dad around and put him on the right road. But ever since that he's had a thing about roundabouts. Every Tuesday, dad will head into nearby Cross Hands where he'll have a bit of breakfast, do some shopping and then play bingo at the workingmen's club in the afternoon. If he needs to pop to Aldi or Leekes, he won't drive around the roundabout to get there – he would rather walk underneath the dual carriageway, even though it's a bit of a trek.

So, given all that, you can understand my 'stay local'

proviso to Alun West. But what does he do? He only tells me I'm doing Tregaron versus Nantgaredig, pretty much out in the sticks, 40-odd miles away and a good hour's drive from my home in Mynyddcerrig!

What do I do now? As a youngster keen to make his mark, obviously I couldn't say I didn't want to do my first senior game. But I'd been presented with a real problem. Cue a somewhat panicked telephone call to an understanding Alun. 'My dad can't drive to Tregaron. My uncle could take me but he is away on holiday, so how the heck am I going to get up there?' I asked in a concerned manner.

'I know, but don't worry, it's all sorted,' Alun replied all matter-of-fact. Great, he'll take me up there himself, I assumed. That's when Alun dropped his bombshell. 'I've spoken to the President of Nantgaredig RFC and he's agreed you can travel up on the bus with them.'

When I explained I couldn't possibly go with the away team and then referee them, Alun had his answer ready again.

'No, no, don't worry, the bus will stop five minutes before the ground. You get out and walk those last few hundred yards.'

Hmm, it still didn't seem right, but what option did I have? On the Saturday morning my mum drove me to nearby Nantgaredig where I duly met up with the team, got on the bus, made sure I sat on my own as I felt a little bit guilty; I didn't particularly want to start having conversations about just beginning my refereeing career, and duly got off five minutes before we reached the ground.

As I approached Tregaron RFC on foot, the first thing one of their committeemen said to me was, 'Nigel, you haven't walked here from Pontyberem, have you?' Sheepishly I pretended I'd had a lift. Tregaron lost the game 6–9 but there were no controversies and I was pleased with myself afterwards as I joined the two teams in the clubhouse for a pint and some food.

All was going well until the Nantgaredig captain suddenly shouted out, 'Nige, bus is ready, come on.' Now, you know when someone says something and the whole room suddenly just stops, stares and goes silent, that's the best way to describe that particular moment.

The hush was broken by someone saying, 'What do you mean the bus is ready?'

I bolted out of the club and onto the coach. As we left the car park I could see Tregaron players and supporters glaring out of the window, making various rude gestures, mouthing obscenities, putting their fists up, throwing arms in the air. Let's just say I was glad to get out of there!

Lo and behold, we had another bus incident just a couple of weeks later – this time in that Dyfed-Powys Police B versus Cefneithin game that could so easily have halted my career before it even got off the ground. This match was being played 12 miles away in Johnstown in Carmarthen, and once more I had issues getting there. Stuck for a lift, the easy thing was to travel with Cefneithin, given that they were my local side anyway.

This time I was seen arriving with the visitors and didn't the Police team half let me know about it during the game when things weren't go their way. They kept on infringing and I had to penalise them. My decisions were entirely justified rugby ones, nothing to do with bias, or travelling on a team bus, but off they walked, feeling I wasn't refereeing fairly and saying I should never have been given the game as I was from the next village to Cefneithin.

Their actions were incredibly dispiriting, particularly to a 16-year-old who had always been brought up to treat the police with respect and regard them as pillars to look up to in society. Rugby is a respectful sport, but what respect were they showing me by walking off the pitch like that? A teenage refereeing rookie. Shocked and downhearted, I didn't know what to do – this was no way for grown, responsible men to be treating a teenager just starting out in the game.

The police officer in charge of the Dyfed-Powys Police team that day was a guy called Brian Phillips, a policeman himself who these days is the fixtures' secretary for the Llanelli and District League. As chairman, we've obviously got to know one another really well, but we were strangers back then. Brian, to his credit, was fully supportive. He walked straight into the changing rooms, had a right go at the players and told them in no uncertain terms that if they didn't go back out to finish the game, he'd pull the side out of the league.

Grudgingly, they did return. We managed to complete the match and when I went to police headquarters afterwards for the customary after-match meal and drink, having been persuaded to go along by Brian, they were very apologetic about what had happened – apart from a couple who didn't even look at me, let alone acknowledge or want to talk to me.

I owe Brian a big debt of gratitude for his role that day, but what happened got me thinking about my future and, as I say, it genuinely could have gone either way at this point. If refereeing caused this kind of furore and upset, did I really want to be a part of it?

That's when Onfil Pickard, who'd heard about my

concerns, came down to the school to see me a couple of days afterwards. I was helping run the club crisp shop at the time – where we sold pop and refreshments to raise money to pay for the buses for school trips. He approached me, explaining he'd had a chat about the situation with the headmaster and games master, John Beynon.

Onfil started off by saying that when he came to see me after that first Carmarthenshire Schools versus Pembrokeshire Schools match, 'It was to say what a good job you had done.' He continued, 'There was no assessor at the game on Saturday, so I don't know if you did a good job or not. But any referee who goes on the field deserves plaudits because, without you, there would have been no match.'

Onfil went on, 'During your refereeing career you will have a lot of plaudits, but also people saying you haven't done well. When you get the criticism, remember these are the games you will learn from, the ones that will make you better as a referee and stronger as an individual. Sometimes the criticism will be justified, often it will be unacceptable – and what the Police team did was totally unacceptable. But don't let it influence you, we'll deal with them.'

I went home that afternoon, told my dad what Onfil had said, and he provided further words of encouragement which put things into perspective.

'Remember what that grandparent told you after your very first game, how well you'd done, how bright the future could be – that's what you need to focus on, not what the Police players did.'

After thinking about it, I realised dad and Onfil were right. Stuff it, I decided, I wasn't going to give up refereeing just because of this. Instead, I was extra determined to make a success of it. However, there was one condition. No more bus trips please, I implored Alun West. Indeed, I never got on a team bus again, aside from two moments later on in my professional career which, I'm sure you'll agree, were quite amusing in their own right.

The first of those happened in November 2008 when I was refereeing France versus the Pacific Islands, a game played somewhat out in the sticks in the town of Montbéliard near the Swiss border, not one of the traditional French rugby hotbeds. This was the first season of Fiji, Samoa and Tonga playing as a combined team. Unfortunately, I had to send off their winger Napolioni Nalaga for a late and high tackle on the French scrum-half Jean-Baptiste Élissalde, even though myself and the English referee Wayne Barnes, who was my touch judge that afternoon, had missed the bad challenge.

We sensed something had gone on, but weren't sure what, and back then you couldn't check for foul play with the TMO. As Élissalde was being treated the incident was replayed on the big screen and, suddenly, 20,000 French fans were up in arms with loud jeering. I needed to be a bit cute here, so sneakily and without making it obvious, I took a little peek myself out of the corner of my eye. I'd seen enough, went up to Barnsey and said, 'I think this guy has gone.' He insisted I couldn't send him off now, having missed the initial incident and with no official TMO foul play reviews permitted.

'Too right I can. I'm not letting him stay on the field after what he's just done,' I asserted.

So after some delay I called Nalaga over, pretended I'd seen what had happened in the first place, was just waiting to check Élissalde was OK, and explained that he was getting a red card. 'Off you go please.' It turned out to be rugby's first sending off via the TMO – albeit not officially so.

Earlier in the match the French were complaining that a Pacific Islands player had knocked the ball on ahead of a try. When Élissalde questioned my decision, I explained I didn't think it had gone forward as I was on the other side of the incident.

'Maybe you were too slow to get there,' he said, with a big grin on his face.

After the Nalaga incident, and the delay in sending him off, Élissalde asked, 'Did you not see what happened?'

'No, I was too slow in getting there!' I quipped. Couldn't resist it.

Anyway, I digress a little there. A couple of hours later we were officially invited onto the Pacific Islands' coach to travel to the after-match function which was being held at a hotel a few miles from the ground, as transport wasn't easy. When Barnsey and myself climbed aboard there were only a couple of seats left. Guess what? You've got it – they just happened to be directly behind Nalaga. You couldn't make it up.

He was a bit sheepish, to be fair, knew what he'd done was wrong and he'd cost his team as they lost 42–17. Anyway, the captain that day was Sililo Martens, who played for various Welsh teams. Everybody started singing on the journey, as rugby sides do, before he shouted, 'Your turn Nigel Owens. We know, as a good Welshman, you can sing a bit.'

I could hardly say no, so I launched into the Welsh love song 'Myfanwy', something of a party piece for me. After I'd finished all the players stood up on the coach and started to clap and cheer – including this guy Nalaga, right in front of me, with a big smile on his face. I'd sent him off a couple of hours earlier, yet here he was applauding enthusiastically and shouting, 'Good on you, Nigel.' Bizarre, eh! Somehow you can't envisage too many red-carded footballers doing something similar – or being placed in that position with the referee who'd just given them their marching orders!

Bus trip number two came in the spring of 2015 when Connacht met Ulster in the PRO12 and fortunately finished with a smile once more when it could most certainly have led to aggravation. The background to this one centred around Connacht's passionate coach Pat Lam, the 34-times capped Samoan international who more recently has done a fabulous job in helping Bristol Bears' rise in the English Premiership and who oversaw their European Challenge Cup final triumph over French aristocrats Toulon in 2020.

Lam had seen his Connacht side lose 18–17 to Cardiff Blues just two matches earlier, the decisive score coming in the 88th minute after Scottish referee Lloyd Linton awarded a late penalty which prolonged the game. Having seen his team have victory snatched away at the end, Lam's emotions were running high and he let fly at his post-match press conference. The subject of his ire was Welsh official Leighton Hodges, who as touch judge apparently had advised Linton to award the penalty for hands in the ruck.

In having his rant, Lam brought up an incident from a couple of months earlier, when Hodges himself had refereed Connacht's 13–16 home defeat to Edinburgh. Leighton had got to the ground a little bit later than the other officials and his parking space was taken. A Connacht steward politely told him he would need to park elsewhere and walk up because it was full.

As a joke, and only as a joke I must stress, Leighton supposedly said, 'You haven't got a parking space for the referee? I will have to give a couple of penalties against you then!'

Given Connacht lost that one narrowly, then were beaten in the 88th minute by what they felt was a dubious call by Leighton, it's fair to say Pat Lam wasn't a happy man. He was tamping, moaning about the standard of refereeing, and it was just my luck to be in charge of their next game at Galway Sportsground against Ulster.

My hotel, the Radisson Blu, where I mostly stayed in Galway and always got a wonderful welcome, was a 20-minute walk from the ground. It was a lovely sunny day and I decided to take a leisurely stroll to the game, rather than go by car. Everything was fine, a beautiful afternoon, but as can often happen in Galway we suddenly got four seasons in one day. It started lashing it down, hailstones, wind – there had been no sign of this, but I was now getting absolutely drenched. Soaked through.

As luck would have it, the Ulster team bus passed. They spotted my predicament, stopped and invited me to hop on for the last quarter of a mile. I know I'd vowed never to go on a bus with the away team again, but these were extreme circumstances. We are talking only a few minutes, at least I could keep a bit drier, so I accepted Ulster's kind offer and stood at the front.

Once at the ground, still looking bedraggled and wet, I'd just changed into my PRO12 referee's top when Pat Lam saw me.

'Been caught in the rain have you, Nigel?'

'Yes, I walked most of the way from the Radisson Hotel but thankfully the Ulster team bus stopped and gave me a lift for the last couple of hundred yards. Otherwise, I'd be even wetter,' I replied.

I don't know if Pat believed me or not, but I was fully aware of his unease with what he saw as the standard of refereeing in recent matches, so there could have been another flashpoint here.

He just looked at me, laughed and said, 'Oh well, it's better than getting wet, I guess.'

Connacht lost the game 20–27, another close encounter, but Pat didn't say anything more about me being on the team bus afterwards, so he must have been reasonably satisfied with my performance. Mind, after those early days, you'd have thought I'd have learned my lesson about travelling with the away team by now, soaking wet or not!

From first taking up the whistle at the age of 16, I was so keen to learn that I took on board lots of helpful tips which were to hold me in good stead throughout my career at the highest level, right through to the World Cup final many years later. One thing Alun West and Onfil Pickard emphasised was to come down hard on crafty veterans who tried to put pressure on me in not so subtle ways.

There was a lower league Welsh game between Glynneath and Kidwelly. A member of the home back row, whose team were narrowly leading, kept going on at me, 'How much longer ref?' 'Isn't time up yet, ref?', pointing to his wrist, urging me to finish the match. Eventually, when he asked yet again, 'Time, ref?', I replied very matter-of-factly, 'It's ten to four mate!'

Both teams burst out laughing, but not him. 'Very funny,' came the response. But he didn't ask again!

I used the same trick in a far more high-profile match, a big Heineken Cup clash between French rivals Clermont and Racing Métro 92. One of the visiting forwards, a big South African, pointed to his wrist and said, 'Nigel, time please?'

'It's ten past seven,' I immediately replied.

'I should have known better than to ask that,' he smiled. At least he saw the funny side.

A couple of rugby-mad brothers from Pontyberem, Humphrey and Eldon Lewis, also helped early on. Humphrey, who played for Llanelli, watched me referee a school match his son was involved in and noticed how I'd stopped the game after some pretty minor scuffle, warning the two players they'd be off next time. He told me afterwards I'd refereed well, but cited a bit of aggro off the ball between him and a Neath player once, explaining the referee let the incident go, then tapped him on the shoulder whilst running towards the next lineout, to say, 'I saw what you did back there as a bit of retaliation. I don't want to see it again, next time I will act.'

Humphrey argued that that approach gives a referee greater respect, and it became a huge part of my own career. Yes, there have been high-profile telling-offs that went viral on social media, but what you don't see are the hundreds of times I've spotted something, kept my counsel, but at the next break of play I've quietly gone up to the culprit to say, 'Oi, I saw what happened back then, cut it out please.' Or I've told a prop quietly, 'I saw you angling across at that last scrum. Do it again and I will penalise you.'

The advice from his brother Eldon was equally invaluable after he saw me referee Pontyberem versus Amman United Seconds, and noticed that I had the whistle by my mouth and blew it too often. He told me about a former referee from Wales called Gwynne Walters, who actually wore a blazer on the field and deliberately kept his whistle in his pocket. Why? Because by the time he took it out, he'd had a split second to think and often chose to play on instead, explained Eldon.

That was one of the best tips I've ever had. I may never have worn a blazer on the field like Gwynne Walters, let alone put the whistle in my shorts pocket, but from that day on I deliberately kept it down by my side. One of the secrets of top refereeing is not only knowing when to blow the whistle, but just as importantly when not to. Penalise where necessary, but also manage the game in a way that enables it to flow, is fair to the players and helps make it a greater spectacle to the spectators and those watching on TV.

I took all this advice with me into my first major professional game, so to speak, a clash between Swansea and Caerphilly in the old Welsh–Scottish League at St Helen's at the turn of the millennium. It also happened to be the debut of a certain Gavin Henson, who came on as a substitute and immediately showed his class with a dazzling solo try from halfway as Swansea won 59–20. The write-up from rugby writer George Williams in the *Wales on Sunday* the following day read: 'A star of Welsh rugby has been born – and we may also have just seen a star of refereeing, too. There's a bright future for this young man from Mynyddcerrig.'

Gav was certainly sublime that day, his talent oozed through and it was no surprise to see him go right to the very top, but looking back on the game maybe George was correct about the pair of us with his predictions!

I received good reports that day from the great Clive Norling who was head of Welsh referees at the time, and

With my grandmother, Maggie Moultan, and grandfather, Willy Moultan. I miss them both terribly.

In the arms of my mum, a wonderful person and the best mum one could have ever wished for. I miss her so much and would do anything to be able to be in her arms right now.

I was born a referee, there's no doubt! I've got a whistle in my mouth for a bike race on the street in Maeslan. In the photo: Wynn Robinson, Mark Lloyd, Louise Robinson, Christopher Lloyd and Helen Owens.

Mynyddcerrig Primary School. The whole school is in the picture, mind you, with Wyn Gravell, the headmaster, and Margaret Tunuchie, the teacher.

Me, uncle Ken and my father on holiday in north Wales. Uncle Ken was very good to me and and I really miss him.

Starting at Maes-yr-Yrfa School. Year 8 with the form teacher, Mr Wynford Nicholas.

A very proud day, and a photo displayed with pride and honour at home in Pontyberem and Mynyddcerrig. I've got mum and dad to thank for everything I've accomplished. I couldn't have wished for better nor for a different upbringing.

Good old days. Working on Wern Farm with the late Mrs Roberts and the wonderful Margaret Roberts.

The resting place of my mum who I miss every day, and where I always share my feelings and shed a tear.

A welcoming moment, especially after a hard intense match, blowing the final whistle!
(Photo: Sandra Mu / Getty Images)

The South Africa v Samoa match at the 2011 World Cup where the Samoan captain in particular that day, Mahonri Schwalger, was being very difficult and just didn't want to communicate with me even before the kick-off.
(Photo: Hannah Peters / Getty Images)

Always loved refereeing in the Six Nations. France v Scotland in the 2015 Six Nations. Seven months later I'm refereeing the World Cup final.

The 2015 European Cup final at Twickenham, Clermont v Toulon, with my assistant referees and good friends, Wayne Barnes and George Clancy.

Out in the Dubai desert with good friends and fellow referees Glen Jackson and Chris Pollock, pre the World Cup refereeing camp in 2015.

Me and my good friend John Lacey, and the 2015 Rugby World Cup team-bonding camp at the Royal Marines base near Exeter.

Refereeing South Africa v Scotland at St James' Park, Newcastle, in the 2015 World Cup, and telling Stuart Hogg, 'If you want to dive like that, come back here in two weeks to play.'

Listening to the TMO at the game that rubber-stamped my selection for the World Cup final, France v New Zealand at the Millennium Stadium.

(Photo: Stu Forster / Getty Images)

With Dan Carter and Richie McCaw during the World Cup final.
(Photo: Jean Catuffe / Getty Images)

Receiving a medal, well a golden whistle, from Prince Harry at the World Cup final. Every time he saw me at a game he would shout, 'Have a good one, Nige!'

Mynyddcerrig in the week leading up to the 2015 World Cup final.

Mynyddcerrig residents putting up the bunting and flags.

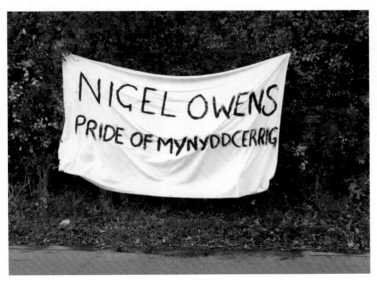

This made me feel so lucky and proud to be part of this wonderful village of Mynyddcerrig.

Three days before the final and the club is full!

Friends and family preparing the face masks.

The 2015 Rugby World Cup match officials' team.

Sharing a joke with the legendary Derek Bevan who I owe so much to. This photo is taken before the Gowerton v Crymych game a week after the World Cup final in 2015.

Refereeing my two cousins, Ioan and Sion Nicholas, a few weeks after the World Cup final and officially opening the new 4G pitch at Maes y Gwendraeth School.

During the anthems I would always look up and often picture my mum there looking down at me.

Shaking hands with Owen Farrell who I have the utmost respect for on and off the field.
(Photo: Warren Little / Getty Images)

Telling off Mike Brown and Yoann Huget of France in Le Crunch.

The day I nearly didn't make it to Dublin because I forgot my passport and wasn't allowed on the Ryanair flight. Thankfully, Aer Lingus were happy to let me on with my driving licence. Supporters for the Leinster game at the RDS Arena made me a mock passport!

An Irish newspaper reporting an example of the vile abuse directed at me over the years.

Receiving the MBE.

In the studio for a recording of *Desert Island Discs*. A programme that changed a lot in my life.

Receiving the Stonewall Sports Person of the Decade award back in 2016, from Sir Ian McKellen and Ruth Hunt of Stonewall UK.

Being given an award by *Attitude* magazine in London, presented to me by Chris Robshaw, a great guy.

1991 World Cup final referee Derek Bevan who had come along to see how I got on and who, as I've already explained, did so much for my own career as a coach, advisor and mentor.

Conversely, the next time I refereed the two teams, the following year at Caerphilly's Virginia Park, the exact opposite happened. I wasn't very good that day, had problems at the scrum and sent off Caerphilly's Tongan Number 9 Sione Tu'ipulotu for what I thought was a headbutt on the former Wales hooker Garin Jenkins. Caerphilly appealed the decision, said I'd got it wrong, and it created quite a stir and a few headlines.

Clive called me in, explained that these were the kind of matches that I needed to learn from and said he was dropping me down a couple of divisions to do Pontypool United versus Garndiffaith. He was taking me out of the firing line so that I could build my confidence back up, before I'd return to the top flight, better for the experience.

I had no issues with what Clive was doing, but after that game I vowed never, ever again to let my performance in a match dictate my next appointment in a negative way. From that day on, I'm pleased to say that I was never dropped down any divisions again.

Just to prove you're never too old to learn, another major lesson came shortly after I'd refereed England versus Italy in the Six Nations and was about to do New Zealand against Australia in Auckland. It proved to be perhaps the biggest regret of my career, and it didn't happen in a high-profile match as you might have expected, but in an under-the-radar Welsh Schools U-18s Cup fixture between Maes-yr-Yrfa and Gowerton.

Three days earlier I'd refereed a cracking Heineken Cup

quarter-final clash between Wasps and Leinster. There was some real stellar talent on the field: Danny Cipriani, James Haskell, Lawrence Dallaglio, Rob Kearney, Jamie Heaslip amongst them. It was a brilliant game of rugby, Wasps emerging victorious and going on to win the trophy that year.

I'd agreed to do the schools game the following Wednesday, but I was far too blasé about it. I turned up with completely the wrong attitude, thinking I was above the match and didn't really make much of an effort. Indeed, I was terrible and ended up sending off a Gowerton player – which was entirely down to my own inability that afternoon as I'd let too many things go. I take total blame, it was my fault, not his.

As I was walking off at the end, a grandparent of one of the other Gowerton players approached me.

'Nigel, well done on Sunday. What a brilliant game of rugby. I watched the match, you refereed it really well.'

But then he added some words which really struck a chord.

'Just remember, though, that for these young players here today this is their Wasps versus Leinster game, too.'

That's all he said, but the message was loud and clear. As I got back to the changing room I thought about it and I just knew that this old guy was right. Of course, school games are different to big Heineken Cup knockout clashes, or Six Nations matches, but what this taught me loud and clear is that you still need to go into every match with the right attitude. The players on the field, whoever they are, whatever the level, deserve that respect from you. Thereafter, I tried to make sure I approached any fixture I refereed, including school, youth, amateur and lower level ones, as if it was a top international clash in terms of my mindset.

I didn't know who that Gowerton youngster was that day, but quite a few years later I was in Swansea's Wind Street, the city's main nightlife area, when a guy approached me out of the blue. 'You don't remember me, do you?' he started. 'I was the player you sent off in that Maes-yr-Yrfa and Gowerton schools match.' We shook hands, I apologised, bought him a pint and we had a chat and a smile about it all. If he's reading this book I want to say sorry to him again. That red card was my biggest regret in rugby. It wasn't his fault, it was mine for not refereeing the game properly. Oh, and by the way, it's your round next time!

Mind you, there was one incident which no advice from anybody could have possibly prepared me for, and it happened up at Gilfach Goch, the Rhondda Valleys club where I was refereeing for the first and only time. Twenty minutes into the second half one of the home back-row players approached me to say, 'Ref, will you let me know when there are five minutes left please?'

No problem, I replied, only to then start wondering what does he want to know that for? I began to worry, was he planning to lump someone, get sent off? But I knew it would have little impact on the result with so little time left.

He said it again shortly afterwards, 'Don't forget the time please ref.'

On this occasion, those concerns having gone through my mind, I asked, 'Why do you need to know?'

'No, no, no, don't worry. Just let me know please,' he replied.

Six minutes from time I had to blow the whistle for a knock-on and, with a break in play, I told this player we were nearing the end, wary of what was going to happen next and keeping a very close eye on him.

He couldn't have been more polite, came over, shook my hand, said thanks very much for the game – and promptly ran off towards the crowd who were pretty much gathered the length of the pitch. As I stood there baffled, a couple of his team-mates said, 'There he goes again.'

Then I realised what was happening. Suddenly, a couple of policemen appeared, wearing those pointed helmets, and started racing after him. He knew they were there to arrest him after the game, and was legging it first. It was like a scene from the old *Benny Hill Show*. One of the policemen was a bit overweight, his helmet kept slipping, he was having to put his hand up to make sure it stayed on his head whilst running as hard as he could. This player was quick, match-tuned, in his rugby kit and had a head start, so they probably didn't stand any chance of catching him then, though doubtless they would have done so at some point afterwards.

To this day I don't know what he'd actually done to be wanted by the police. What I do know is that fortunately for me that was never to happen again – certainly not at Twickenham, Murrayfield, Stade de France, Principality Stadium or Eden Park, Auckland. Had it done, I'm not sure even those excellent early words of wisdom I received from so many helpful individuals would have enabled me to deal with it!

CHAPTER FIVE

Death threats ... and great games

FREED FROM MY own shackles, able to be myself after choosing to stop living a lie, I guess the real road towards the top began for me at the 2011 World Cup in New Zealand. Then it built over the next four years towards the 2015 tournament hosted by England which was to culminate with the final at Twickenham.

During that period I felt that my refereeing was getting better and better. I was being given good reviews by my World Rugby bosses, was confident in my own ability, and happened to be in the middle for some truly epic matches that went down in rugby history.

We'll come to one or two of those in a moment, but it's fair to say that that period started in somewhat scary, indeed alarming fashion. A letter was sent to me at my World Cup hotel. It read, 'If we see you walking the streets of Auckland, we'll kill you.'

Now, referees are quite accustomed to receiving abuse, whether in person, via emails, or, more often than not these days, through social media, where keyboard warriors are unfortunately allowed to have a field day behind the cloak of anonymity. But death threats? This was on another level again and there was a real air of menace to it. The example I cite was one of a number of sinister messages I received in one guise or another after taking charge of the Pool D match between Samoa and South Africa, which saw the Springboks top the group, Wales qualify for the knockout stages as runners-up, and the Samoans knocked out.

It wasn't a pleasant experience. Yes, it shook me up quite a bit and made the rest of my stay in New Zealand for that tournament a little frightening, if I'm perfectly honest. By the same token, I couldn't let something like this put me off refereeing at a World Cup – and it didn't. I opted against calling in the police, but I did share this threat with my close refereeing team-mates, as well as the selectors, and let's just say I developed eyes in the back of my head over the course of the remainder of my stay down under.

Perhaps those eyes in the back of my head were what I actually needed in the first place, because I hadn't even seen the incident during the match that sparked all the controversy. Instead, I found myself totally reliant upon the word of my English touch judge, Stuart Terheege, and acted on his advice.

So, how did it unfold that day in front of a capacity crowd at the North Harbour Stadium in New Zealand's biggest city? If truth be told, I'd had bad vibes about the group finale anyway, fully aware that there was a lot of history between these two teams. They often produced what I'd class 'dirty games', thus there was a lot of pressure upon whoever was referee. I guess that was magnified even more in my case because Wales happened to be in the same pool, and we were down to the make-or-break last round of fixtures. If Samoa won, and Wales lost to Fiji 48 hours later, then South Africa, already boasting a 100 per cent record, would top a tough-looking group and the Samoans would go through to the quarter-finals as runners-up. A Samoa defeat, followed by a Wales victory, would see Warren Gatland's Dragons go through with the Springboks.

As I've previously explained, I've always been 100 per cent neutral out in the middle, fair to the two teams on the pitch with me. I may make mistakes – who doesn't, we are only human after all – but there is never, ever, ever any sense of favouritism to one side over the other.

However, Samoa weren't happy that a Welshman had been put in charge of this match, given what was at stake. They didn't want me there – and didn't I soon know it! When I went into their changing room just before kick-off, a customary practice to check everything – the boots, the mandatory chat with the front-row players, and just to ensure everything was OK in general, or if they needed anything clarified about how I intended to officiate the 80 minutes – I just sensed a horrible atmosphere. The players didn't want to speak to me, or have anything to do with me. When I tried to talk to the front rows to discuss scrummaging, they were looking away.

This is going to be one heck of a tough afternoon Nigel, I thought to myself. So it was, too. Niggly, hard, very physical, with a lot happening on and off the ball, but I felt I was keeping control. South Africa had stormed into a 13–0 lead, but Samoa were fighting back hard when the flashpoint came ten minutes from time and I had to send off their full-back Paul Williams for striking the Springboks flanker Heinrich Brüssow.

Williams was holding Brüssow into a ruck after the ball had gone, and the South African back rower responded by hitting down hard with his hand several times to try to free himself. As Brüssow swung around and started to move away, Williams retaliated by catching him in the face. This happened off the ball; I was following play in the opposite direction, and the first I knew something was up was when I heard a huge roar from the crowd on the other side of the pitch. I looked up, aware something had clearly gone on, and blew my whistle.

I always had an agreement with my assistant referees that if they saw something bad they needed to say, 'Nigel, I've got major foul play,' and that would be the signal for a probable red card. Quite clear, no speaking in code, we all knew exactly where we stood.

Stuart Terheege threw me though, because on this occasion he didn't use those agreed words. Instead, he tried to explain what he'd seen. 'It's a deliberate strike to the face,' Stuart said, followed by, 'It has to be a red card,' when I asked for his recommendation.

I was a bit shocked by this, but given a lack of video replays back then it meant I had no option but to send Williams off. When I looked at the incident for the first time on TV afterwards, my immediate reaction was I thought that a red card was a bit harsh, it was more of a slap than a punch. A yellow would have sufficed at most, due to the mitigation involved by the actions of Brüssow, even though one could argue Williams had only himself to blame for starting it all off.

Whatever, being down to 14 men obviously made the mindset of the Samoan team even worse. They went on to lose the game 13–5, were knocked out, had an easy target afterwards in a Welsh referee, and their captain Mahonri Schwalger was very critical, saying Brüssow had been doing 'a little bit of acting out there' and maintaining 'there was nothing in that'.

Schwalger was entitled to his view of course, but what happened afterwards was horrible and way over the top. I won't say I was bombarded with hate mail, but I had a fair bit of it. Somebody telephoned the hotel asking if I was there, clearly up to no good. There were death threats and it all became somewhat frightening.

I thought I'd blown my chances of getting a knockout game on the back of all that controversy, but Paddy O'Brien, World Rugby's head of referees at the time, told me that I had produced a good performance in very difficult circumstances. Not brilliant, he said, but not bad either. I was actually handed the quarter-final match between hosts New Zealand and Argentina the following weekend.

Trouble was, that game was also in Auckland, so it meant spending another nine days in the city with the menace that was going on behind the scenes. Obviously, some of the threats that came my way were anonymous, but there were some people who put their names to the nasty things being said as well.

I was mindful not only of Samoan supporters at the tournament, but also the fact that a lot of Pacific Islanders had settled in Auckland, while New Zealand fans had also been rooting for them over their fierce rugby rivals South Africa, who they tended to want to lose.

It was quite uncomfortable for a while. I was certainly wary of being seen out and about that week, but come the quarter-final I had to put it all to the back of my mind and focus on the day job. Which is exactly what I did.

As I say, we all get abuse as referees, but a line was crossed there. This was the worst I'd known it during my many years in the game.

The World Rugby powers-that-be were aware of what was

going on, realised the pressure I'd been put under, and were very supportive throughout. Indeed, they even changed the way they made appointments on the back of what happened. Starting with the next World Cup, and beyond, you would no longer referee a pool match between any of the sides if your own country was also in that group.

So, for example, in 2015, England, Australia and Wales were drawn together in what became known as the group of death. Straight away that ruled out myself and England's top referee Wayne Barnes from doing England versus Australia and Australia against Wales respectively, the games instead going to Romain Poite (France) and Craig Joubert (South Africa).

We'd have done them fairly of course, but World Rugby didn't want to put any other referees in the awkward position I'd found myself in and this was a simple solution to eradicate any such problems.

By the way, Wales hammered Fiji 66–0 two days later – so it would not have made a jot of difference had Samoa beaten the Springboks anyway. All that commotion, those threats ... for nothing, you might well conclude.

I was really pleased with my performances at that World Cup, particularly as I hadn't been refereeing that well at one point in the build-up and needed a bit of a kick up the backside from the World Rugby selectors, the men who make the key appointments.

I'd done a game in the summer of 2010, Australia 27–17 England in Perth, when I had trouble at the scrums. Then, just months out from the tournament, there was a Six Nations match up in Murrayfield, where Ireland narrowly overcame Scotland, which also wasn't great for me. I had a poor game by my standards. There was a reason for this.

I'd had a pretty bad relationship break-up early on in 2011 and it was clearly affecting me. I was also still struggling with my mum's death, even though a couple of years had passed by then. I didn't really tell anyone about this, kept it to myself, but between all of this and the pressures of refereeing, I was not in the best place during this period and in a bad frame of mind.

My mum's death was affecting me more than I let on. You never get over losing someone you love so much, but as the years go by you tend to remember them more with a smile than a tear. Every single day I still think of her and miss her so much.

We're all human, we all have emotions, and at the time all of this was affecting me in my work, as it might do with other people, whatever their careers. I knew I needed to snap out of it, realised I couldn't be using this as an excuse for bad refereeing performances. I either had to sort out the issues there and then, or I needed to take a break from refereeing until it would be OK to get back on the horse, so to speak.

With a World Cup on the horizon I didn't really want to give up refereeing, even temporarily, so I vowed to sort my mind out. And I did. I also started to do some fitness work with the ex-Wales winger Wayne Proctor, which was of great benefit. There's no grey area with Proc, it's black or white – do it his way or don't do it at all. He really put me through the mill, got me as fit as I'd ever been, helped to make sure I was in the right position to see things on the field of play, and the upshot of it was a very good tournament for me personally. Myself and Tim Hayes were the two Welsh officials selected for that particular tournament in New Zealand, and we were certainly as fit as any other referee out there after Proc had put us through our paces.

My first two games, Fiji versus Namibia, another of those matches in Pool D, and New Zealand against Japan, went well. We are assessed after every game, something of a self-critique but, importantly, an assessor, always a former top referee himself, tells you what he thinks you did well and what can be improved upon. His verdict is key. I received good reports.

Next up was Australia versus the USA in Wellington, a comfortable victory for the Wallabies. My assessor that day was the wonderful French character Michel Lamoulie and he told me, 'Nigel, your fitness is excellent, your refereeing is excellent, you were everywhere on the pitch. I'm sure you could do matches on your own, you don't need touch judges.'

Wow, a compliment indeed, yes a boost to the ego. My other games, that clash between South Africa and Samoa, and then New Zealand's 33–10 quarter-final victory over Argentina, had also gone as well as could be expected.

After every World Cup you have a much longer one-to-one meeting to look at your performances as a whole during the tournament. Paddy O'Brien had previously questioned some of my decision-making in those pre-World Cup matches when that relationship break-up, plus still struggling with the loss of my mum, was affecting me. Indeed, he told me to pull my socks up. However, now he was able to adopt a far more positive tone when we sat down for my debrief.

'Nigel, you've taken on board what I had to say previously. This was you back right at the top of your game,' Paddy started. 'Your challenge now is to maintain these standards over the next four years, go into the 2015 tournament as the best referee in the world, and put yourself in a position to be in with a real chance of getting the final. The semi-final must be the least you should be aiming for. That's what we're expecting of you.'

Talk about flying home from New Zealand on a high, particularly after that little episode in Auckland. Paddy had set me a goal, one which I was determined to achieve, and I think it's fair to say things just started to fly from there.

Matches began to come thick and fast for me. Some of them proved to be epic encounters, and my refereeing stock rose as we edged closer to the next World Cup where England were the official hosts.

That doesn't mean to say that everything was plain sailing, let me stress. Far from it, in fact. I actually took quite a bit of stick for one of the next matches I took charge of, a summer tour clash between New Zealand and Ireland in Addington, Christchurch. With the scores tied at 19–19 near the end, and the Irish in All Blacks territory at a scrum, I gave a penalty against the men in green for taking it around. Now I've always been very strict, and accurate, in penalising a team that wheels a scrum, and I had no doubt that this was the correct decision. Penalty New Zealand, kick to touch, couple of rucks later and Dan Carter bangs over a drop goal with 30 seconds to go to win the game 22–19.

I received a lot of criticism for that defeat from Irish pundits, as if it were my fault. I was even sent a copy of one of the main Irish newspapers which had published a letter from someone saying it was a ridiculously poor decision, claiming Ireland would never have wheeled the scrum from their own put-in and that I didn't know what I was doing. The signatory of the letter was one Charlie Faulkner; it even said he was an ex-Wales and Lions front-row forward. Now, I've no way of knowing for absolute certainty if this was the *real* Charlie Faulkner, the 1970s prop legend, who with Bobby Windsor and Graham Price formed the fearsome Pontypool and Wales front row of that era. I've never met Charlie, but if I did I'd ask him about that letter – and point out that the game, and its laws, have moved on significantly, and what may have happened more than 40 years ago doesn't necessarily happen today.

In any case, the feedback I received from Paddy O'Brien and everybody else involved in the refereeing community was that it was 100 per cent the right call.

To be fair, heavy criticism like that was actually something of a rarity at the time. Shortly before, I'd refereed the 2012 European Cup final between Leinster and Ulster at Twickenham. For whatever reason Graham Henry, New Zealand's World Cup-winning coach from a year earlier, was in the stands for the game and someone I know happened to be seated nearby. I'm told that Henry said, 'Heck that was a damn good refereeing performance.' Apparently, he then repeated the words for good measure – 'A damn good refereeing performance.'

I suppose, though, it was a couple of games within the space of a few weeks during the autumn of 2013 which saw my reputation rise further amongst rugby coaches, pundits, players and the public at large.

The first of those was South Africa 27–38 New Zealand at the iconic Ellis Park Stadium in Johannesburg in October of that year, a truly thrilling, see-saw Rugby Championship clash that some were even dubbing the Match of the Century. Wow, what a game that was – and a bit of an amusing build-up to it, as well.

A week earlier I'd run touch for the French referee Jérôme Garcès as the Springboks beat Australia in Cape Town to set up a title decider seven days later with the world champion All Blacks. Jérôme was flying home. I had to go on to Jo'burg and left it very late, the day before the game in fact, so I wouldn't be affected by the Highveld altitude. The theory is you either go seven to ten days early in order to acclimatise properly, or you leave it until the last possible moment when it doesn't affect you so badly. Of course, Cape Town was also a much nicer and safer location to spend my week at than Jo'burg.

Upon arrival I was fully aware of what was at stake here. South Africa needed to beat the All Blacks, and with a bonus point, to win the Rugby Championship crown. There is no bigger rugby rivalry than this one. It is historic, intense, it means everything to these two immensely proud rugby nations, so there was no way New Zealand were going to roll over and let that happen. They were determined to seal the title themselves. In fact, they only needed a losing bonus point to do so, but that isn't part of the All Blacks' mentality. Winning the title, while losing a match, wouldn't go down well. It had to be a victory and nothing else for the men in black.

I'd put out a tweet a couple of days earlier saying that I was looking forward to the biggest game of my career to date. One leading South African newspaper responded to that with banner headlines on match-day saying, 'Today must be huge, even referee Nigel Owens is saying so.'

I may only have been in Johannesburg for 24 hours, but I was caught up in the hype surrounding the occasion and knew these two great teams would go hammer and tongs at one another.

I was staying at a hotel in a compound in the middle of nowhere. We were strongly advised that, even to go just 200 yards to another part of the area, whether to a bar, restaurant or local shop, we should take a taxi because it was dangerous in that particular part of the city. As a referee, it's a tradition to meet the coaches the day before a game just to run through any concerns either you, or they might have – about themselves, the opposition, how you want the game to run, what you'll be specifically looking out for, and so on. These meetings are important; they provide you with a greater understanding of the teams, and vice versa, giving them a clearer idea of what the referee is expecting from them, as well.

South Africa's delegation came to my hotel first, their excellent captain Jean de Villiers doing the bulk of the talking. What a top guy he is, never gives you an ounce of trouble. New Zealand arrived a couple of hours later – their new head coach Steve Hansen, his forwards coach Mike Cron, the captain Richie McCaw and Kieran Read, as pack leader.

We had our chat and at the end of it Hansen said to me, 'You're a bit out of the way here mate, aren't you? How are you going to get to the ground then? It's taken us over an hour to get here with the traffic. You'll have to leave three hours earlier than normal just to get there on time.'

I couldn't resist, and replied, 'Oh it's OK. I've just been with South Africa and they've kindly invited me to go on the bus with them.' I guess those earlier memories of travelling on the opposition team coach sprang to mind. I was just being mischievous!

Steve looked at me for a moment, half-wondering if I was being genuine, before a little smile came across his face. 'Mate, it wouldn't surprise me in the slightest if you did get on the bus with them! But we're not going to give you a lift back when they lose, mind.'

'See you tomorrow.' I smiled back, and off they went.

As luck would have it, pretty much the first person I saw upon arriving at the ground the next day, having been taken there as per normal by courtesy car, of course, was Steve Hansen again.

As I walked into the entrance for players and officials at Ellis Park, he was waiting there.

'Didn't notice you coming off the bus, mate?'

'No,' I responded. 'I asked them to let me off 200 yards up the road so you wouldn't see me on there.'

'There's no way on earth you'd be walking 200 yards anywhere around here, I've seen your hotel,' Hansen immediately hit back.

There was good, friendly banter there. I had the utmost respect for Hansen. He was always straight-talking but respectful with it, and also willing to listen and debate, with the game of rugby being the winner uppermost in his mind. I learned a lot through conversations with him. A good, genuine rugby man and, of course, a brilliant coach too who went on to win the World Cup in his own right, having been Graham Henry's assistant in 2011. Some coaches were always nice to your face when they won, but if they lost you'd be in the firing line with four pages worth of points sent to you on things they disagreed with – with barely a quarter of a page of it having any true worth. Win or lose, Hansen was always fair.

I guess he just about had the last laugh in our little exchange, and he also did after the game with the Springboks, New Zealand winning a truly amazing 80 minutes of rugby that ebbed and flowed one way, then the other, then back again, with brilliant tries scored, dazzling skills displayed throughout – and yes, I'd like to think I played my part in how I refereed it, too.

This was pulsating, end-to-end, breathtaking stuff, majestic rugby produced by world-class players right at the peak of their powers. Bryan Habana scored two early tries for the Springboks, one an incredible effort, before having to leave the field with a hamstring injury. Ben Smith and Liam Messam responded for the All Blacks. Tries from Willie le Roux and Jean de Villiers put South Africa back in front, before scores by Beauden Barrett and Kieran Read sealed a dramatic finale and victory for the All Blacks.

Early in the second half New Zealand replaced their hooker Andrew Hore with Dane Coles, but the fourth official alerted me to a problem. Coles' name was not down as a replacement, Keven Mealamu's was. I had to go over to the touchline to see what was happening and the New Zealand team manager was terribly apologetic, saying he had written down the wrong name by mistake. I called the two captains over, Richie McCaw and Jean de Villiers, and told them as far as I was concerned this was a genuine innocent error and I felt we should just proceed with Coles coming on.

'Yes, it's a cracking game of rugby, let's just get on with it,' de Villiers responded. Credit to the Springboks' skipper, he could have kicked up a fuss, refused permission and left the All Blacks in a bit of a hole with front-row issues, but the match was played in the right spirit on and off the pitch.

I'm still not entirely sure how I kept up with the frenetic pace. I guess that fitness work I'd done with Wayne Proctor, and later with our new fitness coach Matthew Evans, was bearing dividends. But ten minutes from the end the altitude took its toll on me when South Africa broke away from a lineout and I found myself running at full pelt near the touchline, desperately trying to keep up with one of their wingers. In doing so, probably because of the relentless nature of the previous 70 minutes, I suddenly felt cramp in my calf and had to go to ground injured as the ball went out of play. One of my touch judges also happened to be my good friend John Lacey, the Irish official who reckoned he was the fastest referee around – and, as a former winger himself for Munster, he probably was, too. John had been frantically trying to keep up with play himself and he could now see I had a bit of a problem, the physio coming on to treat me. Knowing what a fabulous game it was, John was telling me, 'Don't risk it Nige,' even trying to physically drag me off the pitch as he spoke.

I told him, 'There is no way on earth I'm coming off here and giving you credit for this game by taking over just for the last ten minutes!'

We laughed. Somehow I managed to see the remaining time out, and afterwards I walked into a hospitality room that was packed with South African supporters. Their team had just lost to their huge rivals, remember, yet as I entered everyone just started clapping.

That's when I realised just how good those 80 minutes must have been for everybody watching. They wouldn't let me leave until I'd had a few drinks and joined in a good old sing-song. It was only after I'd done a solo – the Welsh song 'Myfanwy', what else – that I could finally head back to my hotel. By courtesy of our official match officials' transport, of course!

The publicity that followed was incredible, right across

the world. Everything just went mental, lots of pundits were saying it was the best game of rugby they had seen, the Match of the Century phrase was coined, and I was getting a lot of the credit, too. ESPN even had me down as the 'Hero of the Game', their report saying, 'He looked shot at the end, even went down with cramp, but you can't blame him. The match was played at a relentless pace and Owens did not put a foot wrong. If Wales fail to get to the 2015 World Cup final, Owens will be there.'

Others were beginning to say similar kind things. I felt on top of the world. Which was better than being poleaxed on the ground at the bottom of a ruck I suppose, which is where I found myself during a previous New Zealand versus South Africa showdown in August 2010 – two sets of big brutes of forwards piling in on top of me. No doubt to the amusement of themselves, and also the crowd watching that day at Soccer City in Johannesburg.

This was another occasion to behold, the first time the Springboks had appeared at the newly-built stadium in Soweto, home of so many black townships, and where Spain had beaten the Netherlands in extra time just a month earlier to win the 2010 football World Cup.

What an honour it was to be at this incredible ground. There were 94,000 packed inside, creating a raucous atmosphere, even if the All Blacks spoiled the home party by edging a 22–29 thriller to snatch the Tri-Nations title from their old foes, thanks to Richie McCaw and Israel Dagg tries in the last two minutes.

Another epic match, although this time I guess the day became famous for two other reasons. One was the landmark 100th Test cap for South Africa's captain John Smit, a real rugby warrior and a great guy with it, someone I always found to be hugely respectful even though he played rugby right at the coalface. Smit was up there as one of the best captains I had the privilege of refereeing. The other reason, which unfortunately for me went viral on social media, was yours truly being rather embarrassingly bundled over, a bit of a tackling pincer movement involving the Springboks' hard-as-nails flankers Juan Smith and Schalk Burger.

What happened was this. New Zealand's Number 9 Jimmy Cowan broke away from a maul and used me as a decoy to try to race clear of would-be Springbok tacklers. I got myself into a bad position, right between Smith and Cowan, and the South African back rower pushed me out of the way – and straight into Cowan. Instantaneously, Burger arrived to tackle Cowan, and thus me; at the same time, other South African and New Zealand forwards piled in and I ended up on the floor with players on top of me.

You can see the incident for yourself on YouTube, where the commentator utters the line, 'Better blow your whistle, sir. That's nasty, there's not much of him. He's got a few grass stains on that nice white top.'

The players stopped when they realised what had happened. The New Zealand lock Brad Thorn was the first across to check if I was OK. I'd taken a right bang to my neck and shoulder, and the medics had to come on to treat me. I got to my feet and the stadium started to clap and cheer because I was OK.

I can laugh about it now as I write these words, but it damn well hurt at the time, let me tell you. I've witnessed quite a few big hits close-up during my time as a referee and they all make me wince, but I always say that this was the biggest one of the lot. Burger was without doubt one of the toughest tacklers the game has ever seen and I copped the full force of his 18 stones of muscle that afternoon, with the weight of a few other players thrown in for good measure on top. That'll teach me to get into better positions, I thought to myself.

I loved refereeing those Springboks versus All Blacks matches. I took charge of five of them in total and always marvelled at the special rivalry, which for me matches Wales versus England as the greatest in the game. New Zealand and South Africa are two true rugby powerhouses. They've played one another since the 1920s, have incredible history and, as such, the games always had an edge to them. They could sometimes be very difficult to manage, but they were normally wonderful matches, with a Tri-Nations or Rugby Championship title often riding on the outcome of the game I was in charge of.

I quickly discovered there was also plenty of drama whenever I seemed to be in charge of the All Blacks against Ireland, too. One month after doing the so-called Match of the Century in 2013, I was refereeing New Zealand once more, this time at Dublin's Aviva Stadium in an autumn international. At the end of the customary pre-match coaches' meeting, this time it was Richie McCaw, rather than Steve Hansen, who turned to me to say something.

'Let's hope we can have another great game like the one against South Africa,' he stated.

'Richie, you'll never see, or play, in a game like that again,' I replied.

Well how wrong was I! If this follow-up wasn't quite as good, it certainly wasn't far behind. In front of a capacity and fervent Dublin crowd, Ireland simply blew New Zealand away in the opening 20 minutes, scoring three quick tries through Conor Murray, Rory Best and Rob Kearney – how many teams do that to the All Blacks? Kearney, as I recall, ran from his own 22-metre line to score a dazzling solo effort.

New Zealand fought back with scores of their own from Julian Savea and Ben Franks, but Ireland were still leading 22–17 with 80 minutes showing on the stadium clock. At this point they had never beaten the All Blacks in 109 years of trying. Finally, the moment appeared to have arrived and the fans were understandably going absolutely potty.

Cue a late twist. Unfortunately for him, Irish prop Jack McGrath went off his feet at a ruck. I had to award a penalty, and a relentless All Blacks assault inside the Irish 22 finished with Ryan Crotty diving over in the left corner with 81 minutes and 24 seconds gone on the clock.

What an incredible ending to a stupendous game. It was now 22–22 as New Zealand fly-half Aaron Cruden lined up his difficult conversion. He was wide of the posts with the kick, but I'd noticed that Ireland, desperate now to at least secure a draw, had charged too early to try to put Cruden off.

So I ordered a retake.

Now, what's important here is that earlier in the game, after one of New Zealand's tries, I had to speak to two of the Irish players, Tommy Bowe and Luke Fitzgerland, about doing precisely the same thing then. On that occasion Cruden had scored the conversion so I let it go, but I told them, 'You can't do that. If it happens again and he misses he'll be taking it again.'

So when Fitzgerald led an early charge again, I didn't blow the final whistle for 22–22. Instead, I told Cruden to retake the conversion.

In the circumstances, in the frenzied atmosphere, it was an incredibly tough decision to make, but what you cannot do as a referee is let the sense of occasion affect your thought process. I was fully aware of what was at stake here. This was the last chance for two genuine Ireland greats, Brian O'Driscoll and Paul O'Connell, to get a good result against the All Blacks. O'Driscoll was to retire shortly afterwards, the end of a magnificent 141-cap Test career that perhaps marked him down as the finest Irish player in history.

Thus, there were plenty of emotions swirling around, pretty much everyone in the world watching the game that day would have been rooting for an historic first-ever Ireland victory over New Zealand – except, of course, All Blacks fans. There was theatre, drama, poetry and the easiest thing in the world to do would have been to turn a blind eye, not penalise McGrath in the first place and certainly ignore the early Irish charge at Cruden, blow the final whistle and let an epic game finish as a draw.

That would have been the easy course for me to take; it would also have been completely the wrong thing to do. I'd have been cheating – cheating myself, cheating New Zealand and cheating the game of rugby. Yes, nobody would have been talking about me and my decision-making afterwards, which would have been nice, but the popular decisions are seldom the correct ones. I get annoyed at referees who don't want to make the tough calls just because they are fearful of the spotlight being placed on them and the criticism that might ensue. I tell other referees that they're not doing their job properly in those circumstances. It's not the referee who costs a team a game, it's the team that infringes, not you – but you will cost a team a game if you don't referee it properly. In fact, a few of the Irish players told me afterwards, 'It's not your fault, Nigel. Luke shouldn't have charged early. You had warned him earlier on.'

This time Cruden's kick went smack bang through the middle of the posts and New Zealand had won 22–24.

The Aviva Stadium is a wonderful venue for rugby. I've been privileged to referee there many times, the Irish fans are always passionate in support of their team, but also fair and completely respectful. Very much like Welsh fans, I'd say. On that particular day, probably because of the emotion surrounding the O'Driscoll and O'Connell swansongs against New Zealand, plus the fact that Ireland played so well and came so close to beating the All Blacks for the first time, the atmosphere was even louder and more vibrant than normal. The match was played out to a cacophony of noise throughout, it was bedlam at times. Suddenly, as I blew the final whistle after Cruden's successful retake, that hubbub of vibrancy turned into an eerie silence. No-one was booing, I must stress, but 51,000 fans were completely hushed as I walked off and back into the changing room.

There, the former Irish referee Donal Courtney, then one of the World Rugby selectors and a bigwig in European rugby, greeted me to say, 'Well done, Nigel. Brilliantly refereed. What a game.'

David McHugh, another top Irish official, who would become my refereeing coach later on, echoed those words and also said, 'That's the best I've seen you referee so far.'

Others were also coming in to congratulate me, saying what a brave, but correct decision I'd made at the end. I just said to Donal, 'Do me a favour, please don't give me Ireland versus New Zealand again in a hurry!' First that incident in Addington, Christchurch, I spoke of earlier with

Dan Carter's late drop goal to win the game, now this one.

'I can't take much more of this!' I told Donal.

I was only joking of course, well semi-joking anyhow, but as it happens I didn't actually referee the two teams again until they met in the 2019 World Cup quarter-finals. That day New Zealand won at a canter, there was to be no last-gasp drama for a change.

After speaking to Donal, getting showered and changed, I went upstairs to the hospitality area where the players and dignitaries had gathered, and Paul O'Connell said a few words. As the home captain, O'Driscoll would normally have taken on those duties, but he had to go off with concussion during the game and, I think, was still being assessed. O'Connell would have been distraught, his side having just had a dramatic victory snatched away in this titanic encounter, but to his credit he stood up there in front of everybody to say, 'I know we lost, but I'd like to thank Nigel Owens for refereeing the game so well. I always enjoy having him in charge. We know we're in for a good game with you Nigel. So thank you very much, there are no complaints from us at all.'

Fair play to O'Connell. In that moment he demonstrated the qualities that made him such a great captain and human being, as well as being a legendary player. What a guy, I have the utmost respect for him. To act in that manner, when he was clearly still feeling the raw hurt of such an agonising loss, just showed the measure of the man.

As for myself, I was on the crest of a wave, in top form heading towards 2015. Could I really justify all those kind words coming my way about potentially doing the World Cup final by actually reaching the very summit of my profession?

CHAPTER SIX

Towards the
top of the world

OCTOBER 31ST, 2015. A date that will always be etched on my memory for ever. And not because of the usual local kids' trick-or-treat visits to the front door frightening the heck out of me!

This was the date of the World Cup final at Twickenham: New Zealand and Australia, two genuinely great teams combining to produce a wonderful showpiece, possibly the best final in the tournament's history in front of 80,000 enthralled spectators.

Globally, I'm told, there was a live television audience of 500 million at the culmination of what World Rugby chairman Bernard Lapasset, the highly-respected French administrator, described as the biggest and most successful World Cup of the lot. It was the most competitive, best attended, with the highest TV viewing figures, and was the most commercially successful in terms of record ticket sales and other revenue streams.

Prince Harry presented the gold trophy to the All Blacks' victorious and legendary captain Richie McCaw. English soprano Laura Wright beautifully sang the iconic 'World in

Union' tournament theme song, and the two anthems were truly wonderful.

And there, slap-bang in the middle of all this glitz, glamour, pomp, pageantry and mind-bogglingly famous personalities was a boy from a council estate in the little west Wales village of Mynyddcerrig. To say this was without doubt the proudest moment of my career would be something of a ridiculous understatement. It was that, of course, but so, so much more as well. It meant everything not only to me but also to my friends and family, those who had supported me on the refereeing journey and helped me through the dark days when I'd tried to take my own life 19 years earlier.

Back then I was in my mid-twenties, feeling as low as anybody could possibly go. But on that day in October 2015 I was 44 and on top of the world. Although I couldn't be there, my home village had something of a full-on carnival for a week when they heard of my appointment to the biggest rugby game on the planet.

Plenty of reasons to be joyful then, you might think. But let me tell you a little secret – however well I was refereeing, I actually went into that World Cup, even the final itself, with a bit of a cloud hanging over me and under pressure. It was caused by a disagreement, shall we say, with my direct boss at my Welsh Rugby Union employers. My contract was due to run out on 1 June 2016, so not long after the end of the tournament. Much to my annoyance at the time, the WRU's National Match Officials' Manager Nigel Whitehouse, the head of referees, seemed to be declining, or was certainly reluctant, to give me a new one.

I'm told there were a few mutterings that I might be retiring after the World Cup. Indeed, the producer of the rugby show on S4C, *Clwb Rygbi*, approached me after I'd done the PRO12 final in Belfast between Munster and Glasgow and asked if I'd like to come to work for S4C as I was due to hang up my boots, or whistle, so to speak. Myself, and my team of officials, were quite shocked to hear this, to say the least.

I explained that I had absolutely no intention of retiring just yet.

'Oh, apologies Nigel,' he said in Welsh. 'I was at a lunch this afternoon and it was said you might be retiring after the World Cup.'

With no sign of a new contract, I now knew that I might have a bit of a fight on my hands to still have a job as a professional referee come the summer of 2016.

My coach and TMO Derek Bevan gave me some sound advice. 'You decide when you want to finish Nigel and don't let anyone else force you into it. You'll know when the time is right,' were his words of wisdom.

However, it got so awkward that at one stage I even had an informal chat over coffee with the Rugby Football Union's referees' manager, Tony Spreadbury, about switching to their refereeing banner across the Severn Bridge in England. That was the last thing I wanted to do really as a fiercely proud Welshman. Spreaders, a good friend of mine, said, 'Nigel, I will support you 100 per cent and the RFU will welcome you with open arms. But you need to be prepared that this will be headline news. As long as you're prepared for that, then I don't see it as a problem at all.'

This wasn't something totally new, of course. Steve Walsh, a Kiwi whose contract with the New Zealand Rugby Union had been terminated, was offered a deal by the Australian

Rugby Union and became a full-time referee with them for a few years.

Switching from Wales to England didn't seem right though, particularly after the enormous support most at the WRU had given me down the years, in particular my two previous referees' managers, Bob Yeman and Clive Norling. I certainly didn't want to walk out on that, but the stand-off over a new deal was forcing my hand and at one point I was genuinely considering the move.

Now, a few years on and given everything I've managed to achieve, you might think what was happening was a little strange, particularly as so many people were predicting 'Nigel Owens will be getting the final' prior to the World Cup commencing. Some even put their money where their mouths were by placing bets on me, apparently.

The optimistic noises from the outside were as a result of my having taken charge of what became known as some of rugby's greatest games. Like that epic 27–38 New Zealand victory over South Africa at Ellis Park, the incredible Ireland versus All Blacks showdown six weeks later in Dublin, and a few other matches, in fact.

Literally, just a few months before the World Cup kicked off, I refereed Le Crunch, England versus France on what became known as the Six Nations Super Saturday when the Red Rose, Ireland and Wales were all in with a chance of winning the title on that final day. In the end, in the last match of the evening, England needed to beat the French by 26 points at Twickenham to pip Ireland. They came close in a 55–35 thriller that saw 12 tries in a match that, like that Ellis Park encounter, was roundly applauded throughout the world.

A few weeks later I was back at Twickenham again,

this time to referee club rugby's biggest match, the European Rugby Champions Cup final between Clermont and Toulon, one of three finals on the trot I was chosen to officiate. Indeed, I was to referee seven of them in total in just a 12-year period, an incredibly humbling honour. This one proved to be another cracking game of rugby that saw Toulon's expensively assembled team of Galácticos from all over the world triumph near the end thanks to a try by their 71-times capped Australian wing Drew Mitchell.

I was fortunate that in each of those wonderful matches that I was refereeing two teams who wanted to throw the ball about and play proper attacking rugby. In 'managing' the games and letting them flow, I suppose I helped to facilitate that. As such, given the confidence I had in my own ability, and without wishing this to sound arrogant, I knew deep down the World Cup final was mine to lose. All I had to do was make sure I didn't botch up in any of the group or knockout games.

Yet, hovering away in the background was that issue of my contract, which was running out just seven months after the World Cup. It seemed to me that my performances in those epic games, being favourite to land the final, or being talked of highly within the World Rugby referees' department, wasn't counting for too much back home with one or two people of influence.

There had been a change at the top of the WRU with Bob Yeman – himself a former international official who, as I say, was always incredibly supportive of me – being replaced as referees' chief by Nigel Whitehouse. Nigel had also refereed at the top level. He knew his stuff and indeed had been an assistant referee for me during many a memorable European Cup campaign, as I had been for him in my early years.

Thus, keen to arrange a new contract, I went to see him. Which I hoped would be a straightforward process.

'My contract is up but I don't want to be going into the World Cup at 44 years of age thinking this is my last one. I want to carry on for the 2019 tournament, so can we sort out a new deal,' I asked Nigel.

That was too far away, I was told, along with if things went well for me and I landed the final, I might even decide I wanted to go out on a high and finish in any case. Or if things didn't go well, then I might decide to hang up my whistle anyway. I made it clear to him that I most certainly would not want to walk away. No chance. As such, I emphasised, I didn't want to be refereeing in the World Cup thinking I might be out of a job in seven months time.

A meeting was arranged with the England 2003 World Cup winning full-back Josh Lewsey, then Head of Rugby at the WRU and another who I hoped could use his influence to sort this out quickly. Still they wouldn't commit to a new deal for me, explaining that they weren't sure about things, it was too far ahead, they had to think about bringing through the next generation of referees as well.

I understood that, but wanted some piece of mind. 'OK then, just give me an extra year until 2017 and then we can take it year by year,' I said, but still no joy. As such, in my mind the uncertainty over my future was with me from that moment on, right through the World Cup and indeed quite a bit after that too, as we shall come to later.

For the time being I decided to try to turn the rejection, if that's the right word, into a positive. Their reluctance to give me a new deal spurred me on, made me even more determined to do well at the upcoming tournament. I put myself under extra personal pressure, thinking that if I got the final, as so many were predicting, then I'd be in a very strong position when going back to them and asking for a new four-year contract once the World Cup was over. Or at least a two-year one. Then we could review the situation after 24 months.

I knew I couldn't afford to slip up. So the heat was very much on as I did my first match, a Pool C clash between Tonga and Georgia at Kingsholm, Gloucester. This was a banana skin of a game straight away. I was aware of referees at previous tournaments who'd erred in similar fixtures, feeling perhaps they were a touch above Tier 2 nations, that it would be easy, and it affected their performance and future games as a result. It was crystal clear from the moment the draw was made that New Zealand and Argentina were the two teams most likely to qualify from this group. However, this was a mini World Cup final in its own right for the Tongans and Georgians and I knew that my attitude had to be spot on, that I needed to approach it like South Africa versus New Zealand, or England against France on that Super Saturday.

Fortunately, I felt super fit at the time. The match went well, Georgia won 17–10, with no controversies. I was even applauded onto the field by supporters packed into the well-known Shed area of Kingsholm. There can't be too many Gloucester supporters here today, I smiled at myself!

On to the next one: South Africa versus Scotland at St James' Park, Newcastle, and the 'Dive like that again and come back here to play in two weeks' rebuke to Stuart Hogg, which I've referred to earlier in the book. Even Scott Johnson, then Scotland's Director of Rugby, said well done and thanked me for the way I refereed the match. Previously, when in charge of the Ospreys a few years earlier, he'd been critical of my use of social media before a big game against their rivals, the Scarlets. I still don't know what the reason for that outburst was. Perhaps it was to deflect attention away from himself and his under pressure coaching team, I was told by a few good sources, but this time Johnson was fully supportive.

During the tournament we were staying as a group of referees at the Landmark London hotel, a lovely five-star venue in Marylebone, where we would have regular debriefs about what was going well, what wasn't, and thus what we needed to do to put it right. As we went through the latest round of games, I was being applauded for clamping down on so-called bad sportsmanship from Hogg in that particular match.

So far so good then. On to game number three: France versus Ireland, a fixture that was extra special for me as it was being played at the Millennium Stadium, Cardiff. This was the biggest game of the group stages, the teams aware that whoever won the Pool D clash would top the group and thus avoid meeting an already unstoppable looking New Zealand in the quarter-finals.

The night before the match I stayed at the Marriott Hotel in the centre of Cardiff, a five-minute walk from the Millennium Stadium which is perfectly situated right in the middle of the city. There aren't too many sporting venues throughout the world with a location quite as wonderful as this. Given I was so close by, I decided to walk the short distance to the ground with the other match officials and some family members, a camera crew following our every move as they were filming a documentary about me.

It should have been five minutes from the hotel to the stadium. It took us an hour and a half. There were well-wishers everywhere: Irish, French, Welsh, South African, New Zealanders and Australians. I was being stopped continuously for autographs, selfies, sign this please Nigel, sign that, good luck in getting the final. I stopped for as many of them as I could and it was all incredibly touching, but it also made me realise that this was becoming a whole new stratospheric level of interest in me. My cousin Adrian Nicholas and his son Sion, and nephew Elis, who often came with me to watch my games, gave up and headed off to the ground on their own.

'Make sure you get the final, Nigel,' the fans were warmly saying. I didn't intend to disappoint.

It was a good game. Ireland won 24–9 and everything seemed to have gone well, apart from an incident after just 23 seconds when the Irish flanker Seán O'Brien threw a bit of a punch at the French lock Pascal Papé off the ball. I was following the action so didn't see the incident – and my TMO Graham Hughes must have been watching *Coronation Street*, because he didn't either!

This is exactly why TMOs have been introduced, to help out the referee who needs eyes everywhere and simply cannot see everything going on around him, particularly with the pace that modern-day rugby is played at. As the play moves, your job as a referee is to follow the ball all the time. O'Brien was duly cited and banned. I was a little bit down afterwards for missing the incident. Was this my hope for the final gone?

World Rugby had a new referees' manager by this stage, or Head of Match Officials to give him his precise title, in the shape of Frenchman Joël Jutge. He was responsible for making the appointments, and came up to me afterwards to say it was a wonderful game.

'Shame you didn't see the O'Brien incident Nigel, but the TMO should have spotted it,' Joël told me. 'But, to be fair,' he stressed, 'it's only now after the game I'm seeing it myself, as there were no replays of the incident inside the stadium.'

In this match the Ireland and Ulster back rower Chris Henry, who'd come on as a replacement, took a bang and I stopped play so that he could be assessed by the medical team for a head injury. He was keen to carry on, but the Irish medics were quite rightly taking their time.

'Where are you playing?' the doctor asked Henry, who replied correctly to the question.

'Are you sure you're OK?' I said, before deciding to ask, 'What's my name?'

'Nigel,' he replied.

To which the medic looked at me and said with a smile, 'Everyone knows your name – so that's not much help!'

Anyway, Henry helped Ireland win, while Joël Jutge's after-match words to me meant things continued to look promising. Next I would be involved in the knockout stages. Hmm, there's a story to that, too.

What Ireland's victory meant was that France became Pool D runners-up and were given the daunting task of playing New Zealand in the quarter-finals, back in Cardiff again. Amongst ourselves as referees, we talked about this game being the kiss of death for whoever was appointed to it, as no-one particularly wanted the fixture. Why? Because there was bad blood around for this one, emanating from meetings between the two nations in the previous couple of World Cups.

In 2007, ironically enough, again in the quarter-finals and again at the Millennium Stadium, England's Wayne Barnes missed a clear forward pass in the build-up to a French try that led to the All Blacks crashing out of the tournament. 'The pass was so forward everyone in the stadium had witnessed it except the referee,' rapped New Zealand coach Graham Henry afterwards. There is still a sour taste in the mouth down under about that one today, with some Kiwis continuing to hold Barnes responsible for their team's fate.

Four years later, in 2011, New Zealand and France met in the final and this time it was the South African referee Craig Joubert who came in for criticism for the way he handled the match, the French narrowly beaten 8–7 in a less than thrilling Auckland affair.

So we all knew there was history here and deep down we each wanted to avoid this particular gig, sensing it would probably go badly and thus spell the end of any dream of doing the final. I was having a coffee with Clayton Thomas, himself a former international referee from Wales and who was now part of the World Cup selection panel, when the subject came up. Clayton wasn't allowed to tell me anything in advance, but he was always very supportive. Suddenly he said, 'Nigel, if you get a quarter-final, which one would you like to do?'

Thinking this might be an opportunity to press my case for a different game, I immediately piped up, 'Well no-one wants New Zealand versus France for starters!'

I'd studied the other three quarters-finals. I couldn't do Wales versus South Africa for obvious reasons, while Ireland against Argentina always seemed to be a niggly affair, with a fight or two, so ideally best avoided as well.

'Australia versus Scotland at Twickenham would be a nice one to have,' I told Clayton, hoping the message had got across. Two teams who always play in the right spirit and there never seems to be controversy. How wrong that proved to be, as we'll come to in a moment!

Together, as a group of referees, we discussed who we thought would get the kiss of death game. They all insisted it would be me. Thanks chaps. But then I began to think about it more deeply, and realised, you know what, they might actually be right.

Well it couldn't possibly be Wayne Barnes after the 2007 forward pass, particularly with the game back at the Millennium Stadium again. New Zealand would be up in arms if that happened, and that would have meant a lot of unnecessary pressure put on a referee, and a very good friend of mine, who perhaps was not right on top of his game. There was no way they could give it to Craig Joubert either after the fallout from the 2011 final. Romain Poite and Jérôme Garcès were French, so they were out. That didn't leave too many other options I started to realise. Oh heck.

We were handed our appointments on the Tuesday morning before the weekend games. They read as follows: Argentina versus Ireland, Jérôme Garcès; South Africa versus Wales, Wayne Barnes; Australia versus Scotland, Craig Joubert; New Zealand versus France, Nigel Owens.

Everybody turned to me to say, 'Told you, Nige. Told you you're getting the kiss of death.'

I took it all in, thought about it for a moment, drew breath and replied in no uncertain terms, 'Let me tell you all something, there is absolutely no f*****g way I'm going to let this game be the kiss of death for me. No way whatsoever.

I'm going to ref this one to the best of my ability and make everybody talk about a great game of rugby afterwards, not the referee.'

So there we were. I'd set out my stall good and proper. Back to Cardiff it was, nerves jangling, pressure well and truly on. But what a game, what an atmosphere! There were loads of New Zealand and French fans there of course, but plenty of Irish as well. They'd bought tickets in their hordes well in advance, because they thought this might be their own quarter-final. At one point the 'Fields of Athenry' boomed around the Millennium Stadium as loudly as anything we heard from the New Zealand or France supporters present.

As for the game itself, wow. New Zealand were just incredible. They simply blew France away to run in 62–13 victors, scoring nine tries in the process, some of them brilliant, with the flying winger Julian Savea bagging three himself. Even though it was so one-sided, the irresistible performance of New Zealand actually made it a great game of rugby, although I like to think that my own efforts in how I refereed it ensured the match could flow.

Given what was at stake, I walked off the Millennium Stadium pitch as delighted with my own performance that night as the All Blacks would have been with theirs. Far from being the kiss of death, I was receiving plaudits from pretty much everywhere, but the words that mattered most came from Joël Jutge.

'Well done, Nigel,' he said. 'You handled that brilliantly.'

The talk was growing. 'Nigel Owens will be doing the final.' But the truth is lots of good referees were still in the tournament, including Craig Joubert who was about to officiate the 'easier' quarter-final, on paper anyway, between Scotland and the Wallabies, the one I'd made a pitch for myself. Did I say easier? The following day, still in Cardiff, myself and Irish duo John Lacey and George Clancy stayed on to watch the Ireland versus Argentina quarter-final in the Welsh capital, and to support our good friend Jérôme Garcès who was refereeing. When we got back to the hotel to get changed and grab a beer before heading back to London, it was all over the news and social media about what had happened in that Twickenham game, the quarter-final that was meant to pass off without incident. The Wallabies won 35–34 with the last kick of the game, a Bernard Foley penalty, after Joubert adjudged the Scottish prop Jon Welsh had taken the ball in an offside position at a lineout.

The Scottish players were up in arms, adamant it was an accidental offside and should only have been a scrum, while Joubert ran straight off the pitch after blowing the final whistle amid a chorus of boos. I think most of us referees would have awarded a penalty from the position Joubert was standing in – it looked offside – but what I don't think he should have done was dash down the tunnel at the end instead of shaking hands with the players. Although it's easy for me to say that when I wasn't in his position that day, you just don't know how you would react. Craig said afterwards it was to avoid the anger of the Scottish players who had just been knocked out after a gigantic effort against the Wallabies, but it wasn't a good look and, unfortunately, he wasn't to get another game.

Now, in every World Cup there's always a decision that ends a referee's tournament, indeed sometimes even their career. In 1999 New Zealand official Colin Hawke missed a forward pass that led to a match-winning Australian try that saw Wales, the host nation, knocked out of their own World Cup in Cardiff. He didn't get another match.

In 2007 Wayne Barnes missed that forward French pass against the All Blacks. Barnsey didn't get another game at that tournament. In actual fact, he's done really well to come back so strongly from that, but it certainly knocked his career for a few years.

In 2011 Bryce Lawrence, another New Zealander, made a number of mistakes in the view of both teams in the Australia versus South Africa quarter-final and announced his retirement the following year. He cited his poor performance that day as one of the reasons.

In 2019, out in Japan, Frenchman Romain Poite saw his World Cup ended after he wrongly didn't send off two Samoans in their group game against Russia. Later in the tournament the highly-rated South African Jaco Peyper quite rightly red-carded French lock Sébastian Vahaamahina for elbowing Wales' Aaron Wainwright in the face, but photographs of him with Welsh fans then appeared on social media, with Peyper mimicking the incident. I suppose Jaco did it for a laugh, but the moment that image appeared it was curtains. It was deemed inappropriate – he didn't get another match.

I guess my own tournament ending moment was supposed to come with New Zealand versus France. Instead, as we all gathered again in London at the end of that quarter-final weekend, my good friend John Lacey came up to me to say, 'I bet you're glad now you didn't do Australia v Scotland, aren't you?'

It was more of a statement from John than a question, but I replied, 'Too right.'

On the Tuesday morning we reviewed the four games,

together with the referees' manager plus the selectors, and poor Craig Joubert knew his tournament was now over. We all really felt for him, offered our support, but there is not much one can do during times like this, other than be there for our fellow officials. The mood in camp was a little sombre. I liked Craig a lot. We came through the system together, starting on the IRB World Rugby Sevens circuit many years ago. I thought he was a great referee, whatever may have occurred in the last seconds at Twickenham 48 hours earlier.

My own review? There was one moment, a collision in the air, when it was suggested I might have handed out a yellow card instead of just a penalty, but the general view was that I'd got the decision correct. That was the only talking point from the so-called kiss of death game.

'You've definitely got the final after that glowing review,' the others were telling me. I wasn't counting my chickens. Firstly, we had the semi-finals: South Africa versus New Zealand, followed by Australia against Argentina. A lot could still happen. There were quite a few of us vying for just three games – myself, Wayne Barnes, Jérôme Garcès, John Lacey, Romain Poite, Jaco Peyper and the Kiwi official Glen Jackson among them. Every one a highly capable referee. All have had fabulous careers.

The quarter-final debrief done and dusted, after a little refreshment break it was time to find out the last-four appointments. South Africa versus New Zealand – Jérôme Garcès. Australia versus Argentina – Wayne Barnes. The touch judges and TMOs were also announced and my name wasn't mentioned in any capacity. None whatsoever. I thought, hang on a minute, what's going on here?

Glen Jackson turned round to me and said, 'Yes, you've

got it Nigel. You've got the final! Well done mate.' His assumption was that because I wasn't involved in the semis, it meant that the final was nailed on for me. Others concurred, they were saying the same thing.

But I was in a bit of a state of shock, to be perfectly honest, struggling to take it in, make sense of it all.

'Now hang on a minute, I've got f**k-all here. I might end up with absolutely nothing,' I replied. John Lacey was listening and said, 'Come on, Nige. You've just had the best quarter-final review of everybody. You've been the best in the world for the last few years. You'll get it, stop worrying.'

The French referee Pascal Gaüzère, a good friend of mine and who always called me the Prince of Wales, said the same thing. 'Wonderful news Nigel, wonderful news.'

Still nothing was officially said. Clayton Thomas, a good friend, knew, but he wouldn't tell me a damn thing. He couldn't and he wouldn't. He was a true professional in his selectors' role. I can liken it a little bit to when you come out as gay. Everybody close to you seems to think you are, but no-one knows for certain until you tell them.

I've probably got the final, well I might have it, I certainly hope to have, but I'm not going to know for certain until I'm actually told. That night I was in a bit of a state of flux. In previous World Cups the appointments for the semis and the final had been announced together. Not this time. I had no idea what was really happening. The wait would go on.

The following morning, Wednesday, I went for a quick swim in the hotel pool, had a spot of breakfast and was walking back to my room when Joël Jutge, the referees' manager, passed me in the corridor. 'Nigel, you need to come to my room. I have to speak with you,' he said with his French drawl. Oh heck was my initial reaction. What have I done wrong now?

I followed Joël to his room, sat down and he started, 'Nigel, you must know?'

'Know what?'

Joël just looked at me perplexed and in his best English, but obviously with strong French accent, he said, 'Nigel, sometimes you are clever. Sometimes you act stupid when I know you are not stupid. But you are not *that* stupid.'

I replied, 'I know what, Joël? Know what?'

Then, at last, came the magic words that remain ingrained in my memory even today. 'You know you have the final.'

Jubilation – and relief. 'I thought I might get it, hoped so, maybe. But didn't know until you told me, Joël,' I said.

'Well I'm telling you now ... but you must not tell anybody.' And he stressed the word ANYBODY. 'I don't want people to know until after the semi-finals because I don't want everybody to be talking about you refereeing the final next week when it's important for the two doing the semis this weekend to be able to referee their games properly,' Joël continued.

He was quite right, but now the news was beginning to sink in. Nigel Owens, a boy from a council estate in the little Welsh village of Mynyddcerrig had got the World Cup final.

I cried in Joël's room that day. Only he and I saw that, but I have absolutely no worries or embarrassment in making that public today. Emotion just overtook me and the tears flowed. As a referee, this was the ultimate accolade. My reaction was understandable.

Joël put his arm around me and said, 'Nigel, you deserve

it.' He went on to explain that at every World Cup there has been a disagreement, even a row, about who's doing the final. It always comes down to a vote.

'Not this time. We didn't have to vote. Everybody was unanimous in agreeing you should do the final. You've been the best referee since 2011,' he added.

The tears flowed again. I was so grateful for his kind words. They made me feel ten feet tall.

Eventually, tears wiped away, I thanked Joël, shook his hand, left the room and immediately thought I couldn't possibly keep that promise to tell no-one. I had to tell my dad. There's no way I couldn't tell my dad. I rang dad. 'I'm letting you into a secret. You can't tell anyone, and I do mean anyone, but I've got the World Cup final, dad.'

I could hear him crying down the phone. It must be in the Owens' genes.

My dad is known in Mynyddcerrig for being a bit tight; not tight as in mean, but being careful with his money. Working-class background, out of work for a year during the miners' strike in the 1980s, one of seven children born in the 1930s, so he knows the value of money, the need to be frugal.

Like me, dad also couldn't keep this bottled up inside him. He went straight to my uncle Emrys' house – my dad's brother who lives a few doors away – to share the good news with him. He went round to have a whisky to celebrate, but took just a bottle of lemonade along with him – because he expected my uncle to use his own spirits!

My uncle said, 'You've come to tell me that Nigel has got the final and you're too tight to bring your own f*****g whisky!'

The other person I had to tell was Derek Bevan, my

coach for so many years and a very close friend, also in the strictest of confidence of course.

Those were the only three people who knew, apart from the World Rugby selectors, the big bosses and my referees' manager back home in Wales. Now the final wasn't until the Saturday after next, so it was to be a long wait. My dad said keeping that a secret was the hardest thing he ever did. He just wanted to share his joy with everyone in the village right there and then, but he knew he couldn't until it was officially announced the following week.

Knowing that dad was a bit tight, the locals had been teasing him in the workingmen's club in Mynyddcerrig that, if I got the final, he would actually have to buy a few of them a pint for a change. Actually, even before the tournament kicked-off, dad had promised if that happened, he'd put £1,000 behind the bar so everyone could have a few drinks.

He suddenly turned to my uncle, having just drunk his whisky to celebrate, and said, 'F*****g hell, I've just realised I'm going to have to put that grand behind the bar!'

He did though, and handed the money over that very day. On the quiet, of course. Just in case Nigel gets the game, that sort of thing – a nod and a wink!

It was true though. Although we couldn't announce the news, his son had landed the World Cup final. Yet, hovering away in the background, his deal as a professional referee was running out in just seven months time, and he still didn't have a contract extension with the WRU.

World Cup final referee or not, there were plenty more twists and turns to come on that front. Including a possible move across the border to England.

CHAPTER SEVEN

... Reaching the summit

So HERE WE were, the week of the World Cup final. I was bursting to tell everyone my big secret, but still I had to keep it to myself. For the time being, anyhow.

At least I was secure in the knowledge, I suppose, that landing the big one, and being told that I'd been the best referee in the world over the past four years, would put me in a commanding position when it came to addressing my contract with Nigel Whitehouse on my return home to Wales.

Or so I thought. It was to prove a little more complicated than that and the stand-off was to continue for a while.

For the time being though, I certainly wasn't going to let the nagging thought that I might be unemployed in seven months time affect the biggest few days of my career. Quite rightly, I was on cloud nine and I intended to stay there, and enjoy every single minute of the week ahead. I did, too.

The first task was to meet up on the Monday morning as a group of referees in our team room to conduct our debrief of the semi-finals, to go through any talking points or issues that needed addressing, what went well, what went wrong. The usual drill.

It was a bit surreal for me, sitting there knowing that part of what we were discussing would be directly related to my handling of the final. Yet, none of the other referees knew at that stage that I'd got the game. Well, not officially anyway, although deep down they suspected it. John Lacey and Glen Jackson were certainly convinced and always keen to remind me!

Finally, semis debrief over, the cat was let out of the bag as Joël Jutge called for silence in the room.

'Right,' he started, 'I think you all know, and even if you don't I'm sure you'll all agree, that Nigel deserves to be the referee for the final.'

And there it was at last. After several days of having to keep this incredibly happy news to myself, bar a handful of individuals I'd taken into my confidence, here was the official announcement. Everybody started to clap, my fellow referees turning round to offer their congratulations and shake me by the hand. I was obviously pleased with their reaction, but to be honest my overriding feeling was one of relief. Finally, everybody knew and I could start talking about it.

Although I was up in London away from it all, I'm told my home village of Mynyddcerrig went into meltdown. Bunting was put up, flags were flown, a big banner was erected in the street with photos of me, saying simply: 'Congratulations to Nigel Owens, Rugby World Cup Final referee 2015.'

Basically, it was one big carnival that week, the local workingmen's club packed out every night and people seemingly driving from everywhere – Merthyr, Pontypool, Cardigan, Aberystwyth, Newport, Bristol, north Wales, you name it – to see what this little place Mynyddcerrig was actually like. The village had a lot of exposure on TV, radio and in the newspapers that week.

The BBC and ITV went there to record special programmes. Welsh-language magazine programme *Heno* did their nightly show live from the village, with Delme Thomas, the legendary Llanelli captain when the Scarlets beat the All Blacks in 1972, and Ken Owens, Lions hooker in New Zealand in 2017, taking part as they too hailed from the area.

My dad and uncle Emrys were out every single night mingling and celebrating with the locals and visitors. I just wished I could have been there to see it, but of course I had rather important matters at hand and, indeed, my own functions to attend.

The first of those was on the Tuesday night in Parliament, a trip arranged by Lord Rob Hayward, the former Bristol MP who had served in Margaret Thatcher and John Major's Conservative Governments and who was a former rugby referee himself. A group of us were able to watch close up as MPs debated issues in the Westminster chamber, before we were invited to the House of Commons bar where Chris Smith, who had been Secretary of State for Culture, Media and Sport under Tony Blair, was holding court.

As we were chatting away, one of those latest breaking news tickers came across the bottom of the TV screen on the wall, saying: 'Breaking news: Welsh referee Nigel Owens has been appointed referee for the Rugby World Cup final.'

I think pretty much every Member of Parliament inside that room broke off from what he or she was doing and came over to congratulate me. Again, a truly surreal moment.

The following night, the Wednesday, I'd been due to

speak at Bedford Blues RFC, an arrangement I'd made to the English Championship side some eight weeks earlier. Their chairman Jeff, a great character, rang me to ask if I'd still be able to make it, given I now had the final in just three days time. 'Yes, of course,' I replied, the relief on the other end of the line audible. I drove north on the M1, parked up in the ground and, as I walked into the clubhouse, the most beautiful of sights greeted me. Bedford had put red cards on every table saying: 'Well Done Nigel Owens, Good Luck For The Final – From Everyone At Bedford Blues.'

It was a lovely touch and indeed a wonderful evening. I spoke well that night, obviously talking about my career in getting to the final and I received a great reception. But the time had now come to put everything else on the backburner and begin to focus on the matter in hand.

The next two days, Thursday and Friday, were spent doing fitness and prep work, looking at videos of what the teams did in scrums mainly, plus a little bit around the lineouts, maul and breakdown, so I wouldn't be caught unawares by anything on the day. I'm not normally the nervous sort, but this was different of course. So I knew I needed to remain calm, composed and as relaxed as possible. To that end I cast my mind back a couple of months to Eden Park, Auckland, where I'd refereed a Bledisloe Cup match between these two teams. It had been a good game, won 41–13 by the All Blacks, and I was comfortable with my performance.

I thought to myself this is my fourth fixture in charge of these two great rugby rivals. The other three had gone well. So I was just going to treat it like any other Bledisloe Cup game. I guess it was an attempt not to put too much pressure on myself, but deep down I knew I was only kidding myself. This was the World Cup final, it only comes round once every four years. Outside of football's World Cup and the Olympics, this is as big as it gets in sport. Normally I'm a good sleeper, but the closer we got to match day, the more the nerves kicked in. I spent much of the Friday night into Saturday morning tossing and turning in bed, trying in vain to get to sleep.

My state of mind wasn't helped when I received some devastating news about a Welsh refereeing colleague of mine, Hugh Williams, who I learned had just passed away before the final. Hugh was a lovely guy from Neath, a Welsh speaker. We did matches together, either me as his touch judge, or vice versa. He had motor neurone disease and when I went to see him a couple of months before the tournament, he wasn't well at all. People often ask why I wore a black armband whilst refereeing that final. That was the reason, to pay my respects to Hugh, and I know it meant a lot to his family because when I attended his funeral shortly afterwards his daughter thanked me, and said that the gesture meant so much to everyone in the family.

I eventually did manage to get some shut-eye and Saturday, the day of the game, was now upon us. The previous evening the BBC One network had shown that documentary made about me, which I referred to briefly at the start of the book, called *Nigel Owens: True To Himself*. I awoke to a mountain of messages and good luck cards from people wishing me well, or saying how much they had enjoyed the programme.

After breakfast and a light lunch, the time had arrived to head over to Twickenham. There was another lovely moment as myself, my touch judges Wayne Barnes and Jérôme Garcès, and my South African TMO Shaun Veldsman made our way through the hotel foyer towards the car waiting to transport us 12 miles down the road to RFU headquarters. As we did so, every member of the hotel staff who had looked after us so well over the past eight weeks, and all the other referees not involved in the match, lined up to clap and wish us well.

This was it, time to put my game head on and focus on the 80 minutes ahead. In the dressing room I pulled on what I deemed to be a lucky pair of boxer shorts, a present my cousins Ioan, Sion and Betsan Nicholas, got me every Christmas. These ones even had Superman on them, believe it or not, and were a bit battered by now, but I seemed to referee well whenever I wore them so they were certainly the first item of clothing that day.

I listened to the usual playlist on my iPod, yes the old-fashioned way! I still don't know how to put music on my mobile phone. The last song, just before going out, is always 'How Great Thou Art' sung in Welsh by John Eifion. It gives me so much inspiration for the 80 minutes ahead. As I listened to it I put on a new pair of boots that sponsors Under Armour had given me for the occasion, the words 'Nigel Owens, World Cup Final, New Zealand v Australia, Oct 31st, 2015' written on them.

The noise, as we walked out of the Twickenham tunnel, was something extraordinary, the atmosphere electric and incredible. As I stood in the middle of the New Zealand and Australia players, each proudly singing their own national anthem, in excess of 80,000 fans watching on, I looked up to the sky and thought of my mum, as I did at every international match, thinking how proud she would have been at that particular moment, and my dad, back home watching the game on TV inside a packed Mynyddcerrig Workingmen's Club.

Officially, or rather legally, there were 160 people inside the club that afternoon. In reality it was in excess of 400, again people coming from seemingly everywhere to be in Nigel Owens' home village, and to wear Nigel Owens face masks on the day he was refereeing the World Cup final 200-odd miles up the M4. The club chairman even had to go home to get his own TV set because it was impossible for everyone to cram around the one already located on the wall in the bar area.

Back on the Twickenham turf I stood next to the New Zealand fly-half legend Dan Carter as he prepared to kick off. 'Are you going left or right, Dan?' I asked.

'Left, Nige,' he replied, before adding, 'Good luck, enjoy yourself.'

'Same to you as well,' I responded.

All the initial secrecy, all the build-up, all the previous matches I had taken charge of during my career were now in the past. This was the big one, something I'd dreamt about doing since I was a young referee taking his first steps in the professional game, and it was suddenly very, very real.

My final words to myself were the customary, Whatever you do, don't f*** this up, as I put the whistle to my mouth, gave it a shrill blast and we were under way.

What transpired was a truly magnificent afternoon of rugby. Normally Cup finals can be quite dull, the pressure of the occasion and fear of losing meaning the reality doesn't always come anywhere close to matching the pre-game hype. However, the stellar talent on display in this one – including Dan Carter, Richie McCaw, Jerome Kaino, Ma'a Nonu, Kieran Read among the genuine greats on one side; Kurtley Beale, Will Genia, David Pocock, Michael Hooper and Israel Folau on the other – meant it could only be an epic game.

So it proved, and I was truly privileged to be right in the middle of it all, the best World Cup final in history between two teams wanting to play rugby in exactly the right manner. New Zealand, inspired by their legends Carter and McCaw, were an unstoppable force and emerged comfortable 34–17 victors, having been out of sight at 21–3 before the Wallabies launched a stirring fightback towards the end. On any other day against different opponents, in any other World Cup final down the decades, that brilliant Australia side probably would have won. Just not against this particular New Zealand team who were in their absolute pomp. It's wrong to say they scraped home in their 2011 triumph, but the same players, more experienced and worldly-wise, were certainly far more convincing as they successfully defended their trophy four years on.

As for my own performance? Well, I think it went pretty well to be honest, and I certainly earned good enough reviews afterwards. There were two, shall we call them 'contentious' moments. I had to yellow card the All Blacks full-back Ben Smith for lifting the leg of Wallaby wing Drew Mitchell above the horizontal. No complaints there.

The one that did worry me, though, came much earlier in the game when the New Zealand wing Nehe Milner-Skudder threw what I thought was a forward pass to Nonu. I lifted my whistle to blow and looked at my touch judge Wayne Barnes, but he shouted 'No Nige, no Nige. Play on, play on, play on,' so play on I did.

Now, remember Barnsey had been the referee who had missed the French forward pass for a try when New Zealand were controversially knocked out of the 2007 tournament.

After playing on, at Barnsey's behest, and with the All Blacks edging closer to the Wallabies' line, a ruck eventually formed and I heard my touch judge on the comms mic in my ear again.

'Nigel, nine gold offside,' Barnsey advised. We are supposed to work as a team, so this was a perfect example of that happening and I blew for a penalty to New Zealand.

As Dan Carter lined up the kick, they replayed the earlier move up on the big screen and I suddenly heard loud booing from a section of the crowd where Australia's supporters were seated. I looked up at the screen myself, so did Carter, and we could see Milner-Skudder's pass had clearly gone forward.

Oh why oh why didn't I stick to my guns? I thought to myself. This is going to be three points here when it should be a scrum to Australia. Now, I have never stood on the pitch willing a player to miss a kick at goal, but on this occasion I was genuinely hoping Carter would be off-target to spare my blushes and ensure justice could be done. I remember standing there and saying to myself, for f*** sake Carter, miss this!

But, of course, Dan Carter doesn't miss. Through the middle of the posts the ball duly sailed, 9–3 to New Zealand, and on their way to victory. It was part of Carter's 19-points haul in a highly impressive man-of-the-match display, the player many believed was the greatest of his generation turning it on when it mattered most.

Fortunately, Australia's players, to their credit, didn't complain, accepted what had happened and just got on with the game. As I had to myself. The key to refereeing these big matches is not to let a mistake – which we all make owing to human error – affect the rest of your performance. You can't look to even things up by awarding Australia a penalty in return, or let the error play on your mind. You just have to referee what you see in front of you for the remainder of the game. I've witnessed a few referees over the years, and one Welshman in particular who made an error, an understandable one by the way, but his refereeing from that moment on changed as he tried to even things out. To us in the refereeing fraternity, and indeed some of the players that day, this was very noticeable. He didn't last very long after that, within a season or two was gone.

I couldn't fall into that trap. I needed to make sure I refereed as normal. Luckily for me that mistake didn't affect the outcome of the final because the All Blacks were so superior that they were always going to win. Mind, if they'd only won by two points, can you imagine the fuss that would have started up in Australia?

In the dressing room afterwards, as we shared a beer, Wayne Barnes said to me, 'Sorry about that forward pass call, Nige.'

I couldn't resist. 'Barnsey, you didn't know what a f*****g forward pass was in 2007 – and you still don't know one in 2015!'

We laughed. There were much worse things that could have happened, I guess.

Actually, Wayne is a really good friend of mine and I even sang at his wedding. He always said he wanted me to do that because of the good old sing-songs we had whilst away on refereeing duties together – although I have to say he's a far better referee than singer! When people ask if I get nervous refereeing, the truth is I don't. But I was damn nervous singing at his wedding in a lovely chapel in central London. I sang the Welsh hymn 'How Great Thou

Art', accompanied during the chorus by the choir Wayne's wife Polly herself sings in. It was an amazing feeling, and after some nerves in my voice during the first verse I got into the swing of it. Well I hope Barnsey and Polly thought so on their big day, anyway.

Back out on the Twickenham pitchduring the final, there was another moment involving myself and Dan Carter as he lined up a penalty kick, only this time I could see the humorous side. From start to finish the game was full-on, played at 100 miles per hour, with pretty much no respite whatsoever. Near the end, after yet another long and exhausting passage of play, I awarded New Zealand a penalty and was standing next to Carter once more as he looked to kick.

'Are you enjoying this, Nige?' he asked.

'It's a bit quick, but yes,' I replied. 'How about you?'

'I'm f****d,' he said.

'Shhh, don't swear now, you're on telly mun,' I responded.

I wasn't to know it, but that proved to be another of those clips that went viral. As I've already mentioned, a Welsh company made some T-shirts with 'Don't Swear Now, You're On Telly Mun,' emblazoned across them and gave a couple to me. I sent one of them to Dan at his home in New Zealand. He thanked me, though whether he actually ever wore the thing I'm not so sure.

A few weeks later a parcel arrived in the post for me. When I unwrapped it I saw a framed photograph of Carter standing next to me lining up one of his kicks in that final. He'd signed it on the back: 'To Nigel, Don't Swear Now, You're On Telly Man – Congrats on a great refereeing career – Dan Carter.'

It's one of the mementoes that has pride of place in my study at home. Alongside it is a photo sent to me by the American rock singer Meat Loaf, who was on tour in New Zealand the year after the World Cup. A huge promotional poster was drawn up to publicise his upcoming gigs, using an image of the All Blacks, with a leading player from every team they beat in the tournament lying on the ground looking defeated. For some reason there was a picture of me on the ground, too. Rod, Meat Loaf's manager, got the band members to sign it and sent it to me with the words: 'Nigel, hope you like this poster.'

At the end of the game, just before Richie McCaw as captain went up to lift the trophy, I walked onto the hastily erected podium on the Twickenham pitch to receive my own medal from Prince Harry who, like his brother Prince William, loves his rugby.

'Well done Nigel, great game. Did you enjoy that?' he asked as we shook hands. 'Yes I did, thank you,' I replied before walking back down. As my name was announced, some of the crowd cheered – which is probably something of a rarity for a referee in any sport.

Was I touched by that? You bet I was. Our referees' manager Joël Jutge was also waiting on the pitch to congratulate me. 'Well done, Nigel. You can be very proud of that performance. The stadium is applauding you. It's amazing, I've never heard anything like it,' he told me.

Something else I'll never forget happened immediately after the final whistle also. The first thing Australian back rower David Pocock did was come up to me, shake my hand and say, 'Thanks for reffing a great game, Nigel.' This true warrior of the sport, a real world-class player, had just lost the World Cup final. Yet he took the time and trouble to do this. What a player. What a man. What a gentleman. No wonder Pocock has gone on to carve out a successful career for himself in politics since hanging up his boots.

After Pocock it was the turn of New Zealand's own tough-as-teak back rower Jerome Kaino, another true world-class performer and warrior. Instead of going to celebrate with his joyous team-mates, he came over to say, 'Thanks as always Nige, a great game.' He then said, 'I watched your programme last night on TV. You can be very proud mate. You will have helped a lot of people on and off the field.'

I just thought, wow. These two world-class players have made a point of coming up to me straight after the final whistle on the biggest stage of the lot. The highest respect possible to the pair of them.

Back in the dressing room afterwards, having wound up Barnsey over another missed forward pass involving the All Blacks, we were joined by Derek Bevan, whose own World Cup final in 1991 between England and Australia also took place at Twickenham. More than anyone, he would have known exactly what I experienced that day, and came down from the stands to congratulate me on my performance.

'Did you enjoy the game, Bev?' I asked. 'Yes, great final,' he replied. 'But I enjoyed even more my chat to Carol Vorderman in the hospitality box!'

I'm not sure how much of the final he actually saw!

The next thing I needed to do, of course, was ring my dad, who'd been watching the game at Mynyddcerrig Workingmen's Club. Now, back in the day, when there was no such thing as a mobile phone, if dad was out and we needed to get a message to him, mum would ask me to ring the club. I was only a teenager. 'Dad, mum says dinner is ready,' or whatever.

I was now 44 years of age, hadn't rung the club since I was 16 or 17. Yet after all those years I still remembered the number off by heart: 01269 870330. Extraordinary really, but I'd rung it so often back in the day that it just stuck in the memory.

One of the committeemen, a great guy called Roy Owen, answered the phone. The club was still packed but Roy could just about hear me above all the din. 'Ah Nigel, Nigel – well done on a great final. We all enjoyed it here.'

'Thank you Roy, much appreciated. Is my dad there?'

'Yes, I'll get him now. GERAINT ...' he shouted at the top of his voice. 'It's Nigel on the phone for you.'

Now Roy has a loud voice, and he certainly needed it that day. As he shouted out those words I could hear the whole club start to applaud and cheer. These were my people, it reduced me to tears again, and suddenly I got all emotional.

Dad soon brought me back down to earth. He grabbed the handset and his very first words to me were, literally, 'How the f*****g hell did you miss that forward pass?'

Actually, back home in Wales, and certainly in Mynyddcerrig, this was a final where the public were by and large supporting the referee for a change, rather than any of the two teams. I learned later that no-one in that room was blaming me for the forward pass, they all put it down to Barnsey's error. But that didn't stop dad having his say, although naturally he was enormously proud of his son's achievements that day.

We got changed and instead of going out on the town in London we headed back, via courtesy car, to the Landmark Hotel where in a private room all the referees, their wives, partners and families had a brilliant evening, drinking into the night, enjoying a sing-song and generally just having a really good time.

The following morning I was still on cloud nine and just wanted to get home. But I had another function to attend in London that Sunday night, the World Rugby Awards at Evolution London, a purpose-built events venue in Battersea. I was part of a three-person shortlist for Referee of the Year, and I will never forget the moment when John Jeffrey, the former Scottish flanker and then a World Rugby committee member, announced my name as the winner.

There must have been 1,200 people inside that room and, as I got up from my seat to walk towards the stage, pretty much every single one of them stood to cheer and applaud. Remember, we're talking here about the great and the good of rugby: players, coaches, leading ex-stars, officials and dignitaries. It was a truly humbling couple of minutes. I got to the stage and through the bright lights looked down to see the Australian team, their coach Michael Cheika, who had won Coach of the Year, and Steve Hansen, the victorious New Zealand boss, whose side won Team of the Year. I said a few words of thanks, went to leave the stage and once again everyone stood up, clapped and cheered as I made my way back to my seat.

Even more humbling second time around! I was lost for words – and it's not often that's the case, I can assure you!

The following morning, having had close on eight weeks away from home, it was time to return to Wales – and tackle that issue of my contract at some point, which now had less than seven months to run.

Nigel Whitehouse, the WRU's referees' chief, kindly asked if I wanted a couple of weeks off to recover, or would I like to do a local game. I said I'd like to get straight back into it, but ideally I'd love to do a community match next. The following Saturday afternoon Gowerton RFC, around five miles north of Swansea, were playing Crymych in the Welsh National League Division One. He put me down for it.

There was something very quaint about refereeing a game between two little village sides from west Wales the weekend after officiating in front of 80,000 at Twickenham, and I jumped at the chance.

Twenty-two of us arranged a minibus from Mynyddcerrig on the day, my dad, other family members, friends, and I wanted to go with them. So did Rick O'Shea, who did pieces to camera for BBC Wales' rugby programme *Scrum V*, and who had been sent down to cover the occasion. So we headed over to Gowerton together, having a great laugh on the 30-minute journey. There was one heck of a sight to greet us when we got there. Let me tell you, the ground was absolutely rammed that day. There were around 2,000 inside to watch the game, TV cameras were present, and articles were written about it in the Welsh and UK national newspapers in the following days.

The media wanted to know why the World Cup final referee had gone from New Zealand versus Australia one week to Gowerton against Crymych just seven days later. I was more than happy to explain and I was delighted the afternoon proved such a roaring success in every sense.

Gowerton's chairman, Stephen Howells, said it was like the good old days of Welsh rugby, when village sides would play at home to big clubs like Cardiff or Llanelli containing Wales' star players in the Schweppes Cup, in turn drawing huge crowds which would set them up financially for some time.

Apparently, he also said that the players had been on their very best behaviour and it was the first time in a while there weren't any fisticuffs in a Gowerton match! The game certainly went off fine, Gowerton winning 28–18, and afterwards we headed to the clubhouse for a couple of pints and another good old sing-song.

There was a former Gowerton hooker in there, a bit of a club legend, who'd turned 70 that day and was celebrating his birthday. He came up to me and said that that was the best birthday he'd ever had, thanked me and has stayed in touch ever since with some of us. That is the kind of special bond you get from Welsh community rugby.

I'm so pleased that I did that match because grassroots is the most important part of rugby. Without it there would be no international team to bring in the money. If it wasn't for the people who'd supported me at that local level in the first place, I'd never have got to do the World Cup final, and I just felt it was important for me to put something back into the game. Even though I've now retired from top rugby, I might still referee some community games when the opportunity arises.

World Cup final done and dusted, fast forward now a few weeks to the start of 2016 with the Six Nations looming. I'd been appointed to France versus England in Paris, the game that would help decide the outcome of the title. Yet, there was still no sign of a new contract. Le Crunch was on 19 March, and as things stood my WRU deal would run out less than three months later.

I had previously asked Nigel Whitehouse what was happening and he said they'd have to see, look at budgets, but also think of bringing through the next generation of referees. Part of that new group were four young referees whose talent myself and Bob Yeman had helped to identify when we set up the Referees' Academy a few years ealier. They were Craig Evans, Dan Jones, Adam Jones and Ben Whitehouse, all promising and who we hoped would be top officials in the future.

I had no problem with bringing through the youngsters. You always have to plan for the future and I will always be there to help and support young referees coming through, but I also needed to know what my own future held. I had, after all, just refereed the biggest game in the world. I felt at the peak of my powers, and knew I could maintain those levels for some time yet. At my one-to-one debrief with World Rugby bosses in London after the tournament, they were keen to know what my plans were moving forward. I said four more years. As I uttered those words I almost felt like I was the American President – indeed I'd got the expression from when Barack Obama announced 'Four more years' for his second term in office! World Rugby were delighted with my decision, evidently pleased I was keen to carry on for another World Cup cycle.

But I needed a contract, of course.

So I mentioned to Nigel Whitehouse , 'I've got a mortgage to pay. I want to carry on through to the next World Cup. World Rugby want me to carry on, so I need to know what's happening.'

Yet, for whatever reason, it seemed to me that he was reluctant to commit to a new deal. At the very least it was being delayed. Naturally, I wasn't happy at all. Word was also getting back to me from outside circles that Nigel Owens was apparently going to retire. Indeed, I even had that offer of employment from someone high up at S4C because he said he'd been told that I was finishing with refereeing after the World Cup. I politely declined, explaining that much as I'd love to do regular work for the Welsh-language TV broadcaster, he was premature in his approach. I made it clear that I had no intention whatsoever of hanging up my whistle.

I could dismiss all that as gossip of course, but something else happened that left me feeling a little uncomfortable. Given France against England was just around the corner, I knew I needed to get a big game behind me in order to be match-sharp, so to speak. Thus I hoped to do a Guinness PRO12 fixture, these days the United Rugby Championship, a few weeks before to get me into the groove.

There was one weekend in mid-February in particular that suited, shortly before Le Crunch, but Nigel Whitehouse told me I would be doing a top-of-the-table Welsh Championship match between Merthyr and Swansea at the Wern, Merthyr's little ground up in the Welsh Valleys. Now, I'm all for taking charge of lower division Welsh matches – Gowerton versus Crymych a week after the World Cup final is evidence of that – but as Merthyr and Swansea were certainties for promotion to the Welsh Premiership the following season anyway, I couldn't understand the need to put me on it. OK, the title may have been on the line, even though it was highly unlikely that Swansea would finish above Merthyr, thus I questioned the value of my doing this particular fixture. I felt I needed a full-on professional game to help prepare me for the Six Nations.

So I rang Ed Morrison, referees' manager of the PRO12 appointments, and told him, 'Ed, I've got France versus England in four weeks time and really could do with a decent game beforehand. So I'm not sure why I've not been given a PRO12 match?'

He told me he had me down for Glasgow against Munster that weekend, two teams who'd fancy their chances of going for the title, a Scotland–Ireland clash that always had a bit of history and niggle about it and which would have been ideal. But he knew I was needed to referee a 'big game in Wales'. When I told Ed who the teams were, lower league Merthyr and Swansea, that they were each pretty much guaranteed to go up and thus it was hardly 'big', he replied that he was gobsmacked to say the least.

Ed said he was very sorry, and explained that he would have pushed harder for me to do the Glasgow v Munster match. Not just because he felt I was needed for that game, but also to aid my own preparation for Le Crunch. He went on to say that he'd had to appoint another Welsh referee to the game now and info had gone out to the clubs, thus he couldn't change it. 'I'm really sorry,' Ed continued.

Coincidentally, that weekend there was a lot of fuss on social media from respected ex-players like Brian O'Driscoll, Jonathan Davies and a few others about the standard of officiating in the PRO12 in general. This was then highlighted on the BBC's *Scrum V* show on the Sunday evening. Pundits and ex-players were asking on social media why the best referee in the world was doing a community game in Merthyr when there were important fixtures in the PRO12. This in turn meant that Ed Morrison and the PRO12 were now insisting I was made available more often to referee in the league. I, of course, would always make myself available. I loved refereeing, no matter what level of game it was.

My contract situation – or rather the lack of one – frustratingly dragged on longer than I would have wished. At one point, amid the stand-off, I had that meeting with

Tony Spreadbury, the RFU referees' manager who I'd known for many years, about potentially getting a contract under their banner and refereeing in the English Premiership instead.

I told Tony of the issues I was having, even though I'd just refereed the World Cup final. We'd love to have you, Tony told me, saying he was more than happy to make it happen. But he also pointed out that if I did switch from Wales to England, it would be major news and we each had to be prepared for the fallout from that.

'OK, let me think about it,' I replied. Jumping ship like that was the last thing I wanted to do really, particularly as the WRU, as a whole, has been hugely supportive towards me over the years and continue to be so to this day. I will never forget the staunch backing they gave me when I came out, or when I've had other issues to deal with. I certainly didn't want to turn my back on them, nor embarrass them.

However, at the same time I also had bills to pay, had my future to think of. Moving to England did not feel right, but it was close to happening at one point because of the breakdown in communication between the WRU's National Match Officials' Manager and their World Cup final referee.

So, what actually stopped a move across the Severn Bridge? How did my future finally get sorted? I was asked to attend a WRU dinner at the Vale of Glamorgan Hotel on the outskirts of Cardiff, an annual black-tie event, hosted by TV presenter and *Strictly Come Dancing* contestant Gethin Jones and ex-Wales and Lions Number 8 Scott Quinnell, where players and officials mingle with sponsors to thank them for their support of Welsh rugby. I was asked if I'd be OK to do a bit of a Q&A on stage with Gethin for the sponsors.

I was in Cardiff anyway that day to do a spot of training, but realised early afternoon that I'd forgotten to bring my dinner suit with me. So I telephoned someone at the WRU to ask if I could be excused from the evening's event. I'd been in two minds about going anyway, to be perfectly honest.

His reply surprised me. We really need you there Nigel, he insisted, going on to say they would sort out a DJ, black tie, white shirt and new shoes for me. A little taken aback, I thought to myself that if they were that adamant I had to be there, then I would probably need to attend, whatever my misgivings. So I drove to the Vale, parked up, got changed into my new DJ and walked into the function room where pretty much straight away it was announced, 'Nigel Owens, World Cup final referee, come on stage. We have a surprise for you.'

Unbeknown to me, Scott Quinnell had been down to the Mynyddcerrig club to speak to my dad and the locals about my rise to the top, friends and family; and they played the video before presenting me with a watch to commemorate my doing the final. I remained up on stage as we watched this. It was a truly wonderful gesture, touching and indeed typical of the support the WRU had given me down the years. Also, unbeknown to me, my dad, uncles Emrys and Keith and aunty Petula were in the audience sitting in the company of the Wales and Scarlets prop Rob Evans, a great character, who told me afterwards they made him laugh all night. What a lovely and wonderful surprise this was by the WRU.

When it was time for us to take our seats for the meal, I

found myself seated on the top table with Warren Gatland, the Wales coach for 11 years in total and thus a hugely influential figure, on one side of me, and Martyn Phillips, the then chief executive of the Welsh Rugby Union, on the other. Geraint John, who'd now taken over as Head of Rugby Performance from Josh Lewsey, was also there with us.

I got on really well with them all, as I did with Martyn's predecessor as WRU boss, Roger Lewis, another who was always been hugely supportive of me and indeed referees as a whole, to be fair. Gats often invited me into camp to referee Wales training sessions, in particular the contact sessions, and to explain law changes to his players, what referees were being told to be particularly hot on that year, help out where I could. So I'd got to know him. We were chatting away and Martyn quickly asked, before the first course had even arrived, 'What's your plan then, Nige? The next World Cup I hope.'

Gats quickly chipped in, 'Yes, the World Cup 2019, but hopefully not the final again because we'll be in it!'

I smiled and was honest with the pair of them. 'Heck, I don't know if I'll be refereeing next season yet, let alone the next World Cup, because they still haven't sorted my contract situation.'

Simultaneously, with shocked expressions on their faces, Gats and Martyn each said, 'You what?'

'My contract is up in June. I've asked Nigel Whitehouse about a new deal, but nothing is happening as of yet,' I explained.

'That's ridiculous,' they said. 'Leave it with us.'

A couple of days later Geraint John called me into his office, explained that he knew nothing at all about this and would get things sorted. A few weeks later I was told that a new contract had been drawn up and the document was with my referees' manager ready for me to sign, if I was happy with it. Happy? I was over the moon. It was for another four years.

Apparently, Gats had gone straight in the following day after the dinner to say he wasn't sure what was going on, 'But you need to give Nige a new contract and give it to him right now. You need to hold on to your best referee, not just for the next World Cup but also so that he can work with and coach future referees after he's finished.'

Martyn, Geraint and Gats hadn't been aware of my situation. Once they were, to be fair, they acted decisively on my behalf. I will always be grateful for that. I'd always made it clear that I didn't intend to finish. I understood the rationale behind going out at the very top, but my view is that any referees' manager should be encouraging your best referee to go on for as long as possible, provided he remains good enough and fit enough.

I certainly still felt right at the top of my game. The proof of the pudding came when I went on to referee three more European Cup finals, two PRO12/14 finals, six matches in the next World Cup, including an epic England versus New Zealand semi-final, and break South African Jonathan Kaplan's refereeing Test cap record. I also became the first to reach the magical 100 Tests mark.

It was entirely possible at one stage that none of that would have happened. I'm so glad it did, creating many more memories – and the odd controversy or three! Most importantly, it was to take place under the Welsh Rugby Union banner, not England's. I was really grateful to the RFU and Tony Spreadbury for listening to me, but deep down, as a proud Welshman who loved working for the WRU, I always wanted to remain in Wales for the next part of my journey.

The World Cup final was to change my life further – as was a radio show.

CHAPTER EIGHT

Steak lunch
with the Queen

I'D NEVER EVEN heard of *Desert Island Discs*. Yes, I know
that's one heck of an admission given I now know that it's
a hugely popular, indeed legendary BBC Radio 4 show.
It's been going since the 1940s and attracts millions and
millions of listeners. But hey, I was a boy from a little village
in west Wales – Swansea Sound, BBC Radio Cymru, which
is for Welsh speakers, and BBC Radio Wales were more my
kind of thing when growing up listening to the radio.

It's fair to say that the World Cup final changed my life,
but so, I think, did my appearance on *Desert Island Discs* 15
months after that Twickenham showpiece between Australia
and New Zealand. The response I had from appearing on
the programme was quite incredible. My Twitter following
went up 70,000 in one day when the episode was broadcast.
I get folk of all ages coming up to me to say they listened
in and that my story moved them to tears. Others have sent
letters telling me how inspirational they found it, how it
helped them, or their loved ones, overcome problems when
they were struggling.

Of course, I wasn't just invited on to *Desert Island Discs*
simply because I was Nigel Owens, World Cup final referee.

The producers wanted to discuss the much wider path of my journey to the top: the struggles, personal trauma, inner fears, mental health worries. I was as open and honest as I could be and it appears that my story resonated with a lot of people.

Possibly, this was the first time that my full story, the attempt to take my own life, my battle with bulimia, taking steroids, coming out as gay in the macho world of rugby, was reaching a UK-wide audience – and indeed beyond, given the worldwide popularity of the BBC.

Strange to think then that, when I was first invited on, I almost shrugged it to one side, and wasn't in any particular hurry to appear on the show. Not because of any other reason, I should stress, than the fact that I needed to go up to London to record it in a studio, and that's a ten- to twelve-hour round trip from my home in Pontyberem. Things were crazy busy at that particular time. I just couldn't find a window to get to London to do it. *Desert Island Discs* – what's that then? I don't know if ignorance is bliss; let's just say I know a whole lot more about the programme, and its impact, today than I did when I was initially approached.

This, of course, is the show that was then hosted by Kirsty Young, and previously it was hosted by Michael Parkinson and Sue Lawley. Guests discuss their life story, choose their favourite tracks of music and pick a book they would take with them if they were stranded as a castaway on some remote island. Icons of showbiz, politics, sport and even royalty have appeared on it. Guests have included a number of Oscar winners: Tom Hanks, Dustin Hoffman, Michael Caine, George Clooney, Anthony Hopkins, Judi Dench, Emma Thompson, Helen Mirren and Nicole Kidman amongst them.

Many British Prime Ministers, including Margaret Thatcher, Tony Blair, Gordon Brown and more recently Boris Johnson, were willing castaways; so too England football greats David Beckham and Gary Lineker, as well as managerial legends Bobby Robson and Jack Charlton.

So I guess when I was asked to follow in their footsteps I should have felt greatly honoured. In actual fact I stalled, even asked if I could do the show at home over the phone. No, no, no, they said. You have to come to the BBC studios in London. As mentioned, it was a long old day for me to have to head up to London, then return home again, so I put it on the backburner.

After a few months, I realised I was due in London on rugby business on a particular date and could perhaps fit it in with them. A programme researcher was sent down to meet me at the BBC's studios in Cardiff – we were recording the *Jonathan* S4C chat show there anyway – to help me prepare, and explain how my choice of songs were intended to be part of the journey of my life, invoking memories at certain points along the way. It was only then that I started to realise how big a deal this programme was, and indeed the gravitas of some of the individuals who had preceded me as the chosen castaways.

In the end I made it to London and I'm so pleased I did, given the impact the show had. So what were the eight songs I selected, whilst chatting away to Kirsty Young as honestly as I could about what they meant to me and why?

First up, probably no explanation required, was 'Green, Green Grass of Home' by Tom Jones. Suffice to say that as referees we travel the world, and are away for a long time, so this one always provides me with warm feelings of Wales.

Next was the hymn 'How Great Thou Art', the last thing I listen to for inspiration before matches. That was followed by Nicole's 1982 Eurovision winning song, 'A Little Peace'. This is a melody I just love. Myself and childhood friends Christopher Lloyd and the late Neil Williams used to sing it around the local pubs and the Mynyddcerrig club whenever there was a concert on there.

'Myfanwy' was my fourth selection, a Welsh song sung by Rhydian and Bryn Terfel. This is one of my favourites and the go-to choice for me when I'm asked to sing at post-match functions during refereeing trips, or after a few beers down the club. It translates as 'beloved' and is just a great song, initially made famous by the late Welsh singer Ryan Davies' rendition of it at the Grand Theatre in Swansea back in the day.

My fifth choice surprised Kirsty a little, I think. 'The Power of Love', the number one hit single from Jennifer Rush. When I tell people that I had a girlfriend when that song was in the charts during the 1980s, they don't believe me, but I did. We used to smooch together to this at the school disco – and I told Kirsty the song still means the world to me because it's also the last time I had a girlfriend!

My sixth choice was 'Angen y Gân' by Bryn Fôn, which translates as 'I need the song'. This one, I explained, got me through my darkest hours. Without it, I probably would not be writing this book today. The meaning is that if you turn to the song, the song will get you through troubled times. It certainly did for me.

'The Sound of Silence' by Simon & Garfunkel was my penultimate choice: don't just sit there and worry in silence, with darkness around you, seek help if necessary, be yourself. Appropriate then, that my hugely significant eighth and final song was the Gloria Gaynor hit, 'I Am What I Am'. Why that one? Pretty obvious really. It doesn't matter where you come from, the colour of your skin, sexual orientation, or whatever, you just need to accept who you are, be treated the same as everybody else and be happy in your own skin.

The songs were significant, of course they were, but the programme was more about the conversation that filled the majority of the air time. I didn't hold back and, as we finished and were now off air, Kirsty leaned across to say, 'Wow, that's special Nigel. We've done a few of these over the years and this one is going to help so many people out there. You'll be amazed at the response you get from this.'

I was somewhat taken aback by her response, particularly given the gravitas of the TV and radio shows she'd been involved in. Was it really that special? She made chatting about those tough times so easy, with her wonderfully calm way of interviewing me. All I can say is that Kirsty was proved to be absolutely right. Immediately after the programme, and indeed still to this day, people will talk to me about *Desert Island Discs*, explain how much they loved that particular show, how it moved them to tears.

There was a follow-up to Kirsty's comments. Shortly after the programme had been recorded, I received a letter from the editor telling me he had worked on an awful lot of these programmes over the years, but this one would always stand out for him as a memorable one. I've kept that letter and I'm so pleased the episode proved to be so helpful to others. In fact, I can't really put into words how much it means to me to have helped like that.

Desert Island Discs, coupled with the World Cup final and the increasing publicity rugby was now attracting throughout various areas of the media, meant things started to snowball for me. I was invited on to TV talk shows, asked to do adverts, to speak at dinner functions. I found I was being recognised more and more. Yes, it was down to the Rugby World Cup, but it would be naive of me to think that my off-field issues didn't contribute significantly as well.

Why else would I have been invited to Buckingham Palace to meet Her Majesty The Queen? I'd been there previously, first as part of a visit with a group of referees during the 2015 World Cup, then the following year to be presented with my MBE.

When I was asked to return for a third time in the summer of 2017, four months after my appearance on *Desert Island Discs*, I naturally assumed it was another of those lavish garden parties they throw, with hundreds of guests present and the Queen somewhere in the background but pretty much impossible to get near to.

When I arrived at the Palace gates I realised there were just 12 of us. A small select few. Other invited guests included the chairman of Dŵr Cymru Welsh Water, the chair of the UK courts and tribunals appeals board, the UK-based Head of BP Oil, and a teacher who had started up Asian dance schools to give opportunities to youngsters from deprived backgrounds. So everyone was there for a reason. One of the reasons for me being there was the World Cup final, but so too was the life story I'd just shared with millions of listeners on national radio.

The first change I noticed this time on arriving at the Palace was that I was able to keep my mobile phone with me! On a visit during the World Cup we had to hand them in, presumably to prevent photographs being taken inside the inner sanctum. When I went to hand it over again, the head butler to the Queen, himself a big rugby fan, told me, 'Keep it, Nigel. If I thought you were dodgy I wouldn't have let you in anyway!'

We smiled. I was taken into this large banquet room where I started chatting to my fellow guests before the Queen and the Duke of Edinburgh entered. I was introduced to Prince Philip first. 'Sir, this is Nigel Owens who refereed the 2015 World Cup final.'

'Ah yes, I do like a bit of rugby. Tell me Nigel, why don't they put the ball in straight at a scrum any more?'

Those, I kid you not, were the Duke's first words to me. The chair of Dŵr Cymru was also part of the conversation and turned to me to say, 'Well, there you are Nigel. You've had it from the very top now. Sort it out!'

And still it hasn't been properly sorted, has it?

After chatting for a while about other things amongst ourselves, we sat down for a meal. If you can imagine it being Christmas Day, with one of those huge family tables everyone gathers around, well that was pretty much what the scene was like inside the Palace. Only on a much grander scale, needless to say.

I was next but one to the Queen and pretty much opposite the Duke, who was enjoying a half-pint of London Pride beer with his food, so I knew I needed to be on my best behaviour. The servants came in, served the Queen first, then it was the turn of the rest of us to reach out and take our food off the beautiful silver serving platters as the waiters stood by our side. Think of *Downton Abbey* – if you've seen that famous British TV drama series, that's exactly the way lunch was served.

The main meal was steak. It looked truly lovely and I couldn't wait to tuck in. So, when my turn came I duly reached up, took the steak and, as I attempted to put it on my plate, it fell onto this lavish looking tablecloth. Let's just say I went redder than the wine that had been poured into our lovely crystal glasses. I couldn't have been more embarrassed. The waiter smiled, told me I wasn't the first and I wouldn't be the last.

He was very kind. 'Just pick it up and put it on your plate,' he said.

But, of all the people gathered around that table, it just had to happen to me, didn't it? I looked to see if the Queen had noticed – she had. Her Majesty missed nothing. However, she had a smile on her face which did help make me feel a little more at ease.

Order restored, the steak was indeed enjoyable, as was the company around that table, before the Queen asked us to retire to the drawing room for coffee. As we made our way into another incredibly grandiose part of the Palace, the head butler said, 'Ma'am, I'd like to introduce you properly to Nigel Owens. He refereed the Rugby World Cup final.'

'Oh Nigel, nice to meet you,' she said. 'I do watch a bit of rugby, but I can't watch too much as it's a bit too bang and boof for me.' At the same time she made a motion with her hands to indicate what she meant, although of course I understood.

'But my daughter is a big fan,' the Queen continued. 'Have you come across her at all at matches?'

I told her I'd met Princess Anne, who is patron of the Scotland team, on a couple of occasions. She had been presented to the two sets of players and match officials on the pitch ahead of matches up at Murrayfield, and also at the World Cup event held at the Palace during my first visit there as part of a group of referees in 2015.

'Yes, I haven't seen her since England beat Scotland very well at Twickenham a few weeks ago, so I'm looking forward to seeing her again,' said the Queen. The sport of rugby – look how it breaks down barriers so easily and helps make conversation.

England had actually thumped the Scots 61–21 in that Six Nations fixture the Queen was referring to. We carried on chatting for another 20 to 30 minutes about rugby, my life and a number of other things. This was quite an amazing moment – a boy from a Welsh council estate talking to the Queen at her world-famous home in London. If my mum and grandparents were alive they probably wouldn't believe it, I thought to myself.

After about half an hour of pleasant exchanges the head butler intervened to say, 'Ma'am, the race is about to start.' Royal Ascot was on and one of her horses was running. She suddenly said, 'Excuse me, but I'm going to have to go now because the racing is on.' She moved to the middle of the room and stood there. Once the Duke saw her there he stopped in his tracks and also went to the middle of the room. He stood next to her for a moment, then side by side they walked out through a door, one going to the left, the other to the right.

Again, these are moments I can never forget. Having been privileged enough to meet Prince Philip, I was so sad to learn of his passing in April 2021 at the age of 99. What a wonderful servant he was to the whole of the United Kingdom, a man of incredible honour and kindness who did so much good for so many people, not least with his Duke of Edinburgh's Award scheme.

More recently, of course, indeed as I'm actually proofreading this book, we've learned of the sad passing of the Queen. She really was a truly remarkable woman, a lovely person who had this knack of making you feel so welcome, so at ease, in her company. That incident when I dropped my steak straight onto the table was truly embarrassing for me, but it was the Queen's quiet and knowing smile that made me feel better, more comfortable. Don't worry about it, she was saying in effect. These things happen.

Back at the Palace that day, the rest of us finished our coffee and five minutes later we too started to depart. I almost had to pinch myself on the journey back to Wales. Had this really just happened to me? Was anyone back home really going to believe what the Queen and the Duke had said to me about rugby?

It was surreal. As, to a degree, were the TV and radio talk show invitations that were beginning to increase in number. There I was on the popular Clare Balding programme on BT Sport, sitting next to the legendary snooker player Jimmy White, who I used to watch and so greatly admire when I was a kid growing up and taking an interest in various sports.

Another fascinating one was the Tommy Tiernan chat show in Ireland, unique because he doesn't actually know who his guests are until they walk on set. So, unlike other hosts, he can't do his prep or anything like that, it all has to be ad-libbed as it happens.

Just as well he's so knowledgeable then, and that they're rugby-mad in Ireland. When I walked on to meet him a lot of the audience instantly recognised me and were clapping and cheering, even though my name had not yet been announced. Tommy looked me up and down and said, 'Yes, I know who I've got here. You're the referee aren't you – Nigel ... Nigel Owens, isn't it?'

More cheers from the audience.

'And you're the gay referee as well, I think I'm right in saying?' continued Tommy. Just as well he got the right one! Further cheers again, though. We had a great time on that show.

As I've stated previously, things just began to snowball and I guess my profile increased further when I was given the chance to take part in advertisements, some of which were going out on primetime television. I particularly enjoyed shooting a sequence of different ones for the airline Emirates, who were helping to sponsor referees at the 2019 World Cup.

They were fun! Short, sharp 15-second clips, basically, of me dealing with supposed bad behaviour on an aeroplane, but with rugby twists, and I think viewers enjoyed watching them. One featured an Irish fan dozing in his seat and falling onto the woman sat next to him. I suddenly appear, in full World Cup kit, and with a shrill blast of the whistle say loudly, 'Roll away, get back on your own side,' before running back up the plane.

In another advertisement, a woman throws a scarf around her neck and it accidentally hits the man next to her on the chest. He holds his face in supposed agony, play-acting I guess you'd call it. Up I pop again. 'This is not football. You want to act like that then go to Hollywood. Get on with it.' Shrill blast of whistle and off back up the plane again.

In a further one I approach the refreshments area at the back of a plane and start, 'Can I please have …' before someone else arrives on the other side asking for a lemonade. Shrill blast again. 'You're offside there, boys.' The stewardess looks back at me, so I say, 'I'll have a ginger ale please,' before glancing across to the other guy, 'Alright, play on.' Appearing to be suitably admonished, he finally gets to order his own drink.

I particularly liked a slightly longer advert of a couple saying a tearful goodbye inside an airport terminal, with the man about to head off to Auckland. As they closely embrace, and he says, 'This is not goodbye. It's just the start,' I suddenly appear with the words, 'That's a clear case of not releasing. It's been happening all day. Off you go please.' Shocked expressions on their faces, and grudgingly they part.

The key to these adverts for me was the fun element. They gave a rugby message, helped people have some understanding of the sayings we have for certain rule infringements ahead of the World Cup, but principally they made people laugh and smile. Do that, and you can't go too far wrong.

Mind, there was another humorous advert, this time for the French car giant Citroën, which caused me a bit of unnecessary angst for a while. I'm driving along a country road, jolly and happy, only to be met by a grizzly bear standing on its hind legs and roaring angrily towards me. I get out of the vehicle, and tell the bear, 'We need a chat,' and tame it by trimming its hair and giving it some canapés to eat off a tray. 'Only one mind,' I scold, before getting the bear to play lovely French music on a cello. At this point I look into the camera for my payoff line, 'And that, *mes amis*, is how you tame the beast.' Another man's voice then provides the catchphrase, 'Adventure just got civilised', to promote the new make of Citroën vehicle.

Pretty innocuous, you'd think, and quite funny. Imagine my shock then when a young woman, an English soprano, started complaining on Twitter that Nigel Owens should be ashamed of himself for condoning animal cruelty. She suggested that the advert was promoting animals performing tricks to entertain the public.

I could scarcely believe what I was reading. Me, the owner of a farm, lots of cattle, huge lover of dogs and indeed most animals. I don't think the songstress realised this wasn't actually a real bear, it was a man dressed up in a bear suit!

'Oh come on,' I responded. 'What do you want to do next? Ban Pudsey from the wonderful Children in Need charity?'

This went viral and she had to delete her tweet, but not before she realised how stupid she'd been, I hope. Needless to say, had it been a real bear, I'd have never agreed to the advert. Mind, the young soprano first had to put up with quite a bit of leg-pulling – and inevitable bear puns – from some of my 425,000-plus Twitter followers who, like me, were astonished at her overreaction to a harmless bit of fun.

'I couldn't bear the thought of reading her tweet,' wrote one. 'The next time she's going to tweet something, she should take a long paws and think about it first,' joked another. And so on. And so on. You get the gist.

With the advertisements being watched by millions of TV viewers, with the World Cup final behind me and more high-profile matches coming my way, I guess it was inevitable that I started to notice that I was being recognised a little more when I walked down the street. This had tended to happen in Wales anyway, because we're so rugby-mad as a nation, but I'd also be on the Tube in London and see people staring at me, or pass me on the pavement and sort of do a double-take. A couple of seconds later they'd come back, say, 'You're Nigel Owens aren't you?' and ask for a photo or an autograph.

I always try to oblige and I'm touched by some of the kind things they say. 'What you've done, your honesty, has helped me so much, or helped my son or daughter deal with similar issues in their own lives.' These words mean a lot to me, having been in that position when I was younger myself. It's really nice to know that going public with my own problems has been of assistance to so many others who, like me back then, were otherwise dealing with it in silence. Which is never a good thing.

Of course, there are many who just recognise me from refereeing, want to chat about decisions I make, ask which players are the easiest to get on with, which ones aren't, what it was really like doing that World Cup final. Again, always happy to chat about my beloved sport with anybody. Rugby is nothing without the fans, the paying customer, whether those at matches or watching on TV, and anyone in the limelight must always be aware of that.

As I reflect on it now, although it's easy to say that that 2015 Twickenham final brought me the fame, in my own mind I can probably rewind to a year earlier for another hugely significant moment. It happened 7,000 miles away, in the unlikely setting of the Estadio Malvinas Argentinas, the rugby ground in the Argentine city of Mendoza, in the foothills of the Andes and a 13-hour road journey from the capital Buenos Aires.

I'd been getting a lot of attention in the rugby press for the way I refereed some of the big games, including that so-called Match of the Century between South Africa and New Zealand, and the high-scoring Six Nations clash between England and France. One that didn't quite come into that category, but which was hugely competitive nonetheless and a very special occasion for me, came on 27 September 2014 when South Africa beat Australia 28–10 in Cape Town in the Rugby Championship. The game was nip and tuck for the most part before three tries in the closing moments by the Springboks put something of an unfair gloss on the final scoreline.

Why was it so special? They were talking at the time about decommissioning South Africa's iconic Newlands ground, which had stood since 1888, had housed some of the Springboks' most epic encounters, but which was now to make way for residential and retail developments. I'd been a touch judge or TMO at Newlands previously, but never the referee, so I was incredibly excited at the prospect. When Joël Jutge, Head of Referees, told me 'Great performance Nigel' immediately after the game, it meant a heck of a lot.

I had to fly straight from there to Mendoza where the Wallabies were also heading for their next Rugby Championship fixture, with me refereeing them once more. Indeed, we were on the same 11-hour flight. Now, for whatever reason, I was hopeless that day in Argentina. Whether it was travel fatigue, my lack of preparation, maybe complacency because I'd done so well in Cape Town the week before, I don't know. The Pumas won 21–17 and while I don't think my decisions affected the outcome of the match, I didn't referee well. The only scant consolation was that I was equally poor to the two sides.

This time Joël Jutge gave me a right earful. 'Nigel, I always tell you when you've refereed well, as I did last week. Now I'm telling you that that wasn't good.'

He continued, 'I don't care about this if it's a one-off performance. We all have bad games, even you, but I do care if it happens again. Because when we get to the World Cup, if you referee like that again in a group game, or in the knockout stages, I can't possibly appoint you to the final. So please take note.'

That was me suitably admonished, but Joël was absolutely right and I knew it. So although everybody else points to those other classic Test matches, or my doing the European Cup final in 2015, as the games that got me the World Cup final, I know that that wake-up call 12 months earlier in Mendoza was just as important. I vowed there and then not to let my standards slip again.

Joël would give the stick when I needed it, but he always dangled the carrot as well. He knew I was on top form during the World Cup and said, 'Nigel, you must continue refereeing like this. If you do, it will change your life for the better. I know you're famous already, not just in Wales but famous full stop. But if you referee the World Cup final, everything will go up another few levels again.'

He was proved to be absolutely right, as usual. Joël is a clever man. He knew full well the World Cup final was more than just a rugby match for me. The column inches, TV broadcasts and hype that followed it were more a result of the back story of me getting there, dealing with adversity, the struggles on the way. We were able to prove that rugby is an inclusive and diverse sport where you can overcome barriers, carry on through the tough times and still reach the very top of your profession.

I had one World Cup final to my name – I couldn't do the unthinkable and land another in 2019, could I?

CHAPTER NINE

2019 World Cup

THE FAME IS lovely, of course it is. But, despite everything that was happening around that time, the trip to the Palace, radio shows, TV appearances, the selfies, the autograph hunters, the requests to speak at dinners, the newspaper interviews, I always made sure to remember that my day job was being a rugby referee. That was 100 per cent the priority for me. Everything else needed to come off the back of that.

So, finally armed with my new four-year contract from the WRU, I set my sights on the 2019 World Cup in Japan, the first time the tournament was to be held in the Far East. Even if it was highly unlikely that the powers-that-be would grant me the chance to referee the actual final for the second tournament running – if only to fairly share out the accolade – I still intended to make it difficult for them not to pick me once more. At the very least, my aim was to be put in charge of a semi-final, something that had, thus far, eluded me.

Nothing wrong with setting goals and aiming high for them, but if they say a week is a long time in politics, just imagine what four years are to rugby referee! The next World Cup seemed a million miles away as I took charge of my first international post the 2015 final. It wasn't exactly the biggest fixture, nor played in a traditional hotbed of the game, but there was some lovely symmetry to the appointment. Having done the last match of the 2015 tournament, I was handed the opportunity to referee the first game of the 2019 competition – an early qualifier involving Saint Vincent and the Grenadines against Jamaica.

The fixture was played at a little ground in Kingstown, the capital of Saint Vincent and not to be confused with Kingston, Jamaica. It's a port city, and only has a population of 13,000, so we are hardly talking Twickenham, Stade de France, the Principality Stadium or Eden Park here, I grant you. However, I'm so pleased I was asked to do the match and once I realised the date, 5 March 2016, didn't fall on a Six Nations weekend, I said yes, of course I'd be honoured to do it.

Saint Vincent is not one of the traditional Caribbean holiday hotspots, like Barbados, Jamaica or Antigua. Nor, of course, is it particularly associated with rugby. Thus, as part of my visit, I was asked to help promote the sport by going around the schools of the island with the World Cup trophy for everybody to see it close-up.

The first challenge was actually getting there. The second was getting there with the famous Webb Ellis Cup securely in tow. I remember arriving at Gatwick Airport to meet my travelling partner James Fitzgerald, then the communications' chief at World Rugby, who was tasked with bringing the trophy along and looking after it. There was necessary security of course, the Cup was locked up in a special case. James kept a close eye on it, and it even had its own seat right between us on the plane; seat belt put around it and all. Because Saint Vincent is a small island, we had to fly from London to Barbados and then get another connection for the short hop across the Caribbean Sea to our destination. World Rugby wouldn't let us put the trophy, made of sterling silver but gilded in gold, in the undercarriage of the plane. Who knows where it might have ended up. So they paid for it to have its own seat on each flight. It looked truly resplendent, perched there in the chair, seat belt wrapped tightly around it to stop it from falling to the floor, or indeed falling forwards to knock the seat of the passenger in front.

The locals were so grateful that I'd taken the trouble to go there, to referee the game and then take the trophy around the island. We went to about five or six different schools and what a humbling experience it was. These were poor communities. Kids were running around with nothing on their feet, the old-fashioned desks in the classroom reminded me of when I was at school in the 1970s. Yet, despite the obvious lack of privilege, these kids were wonderfully polite, always seemed to have a smile on their faces – in particular when we showed them the Webb Ellis Cup, which they gawped at, eyes wide open. I even had a few games of touch rugby with them in the schoolyard before getting down to the real business of the trip, refereeing the qualifying match.

It wasn't the greatest standard, probably equivalent to Pontyberem Thirds, if they had such a team. But it was fabulous to see the effort put in by the two sides and how much it meant to them. The spotlight was clearly going to shine brightest on the teams at the finals in three years time, but this was a World Cup in itself for these two nations. Jamaica won 48–0 by the way, but they were never going to reach Japan and were knocked out later in the qualifying stages.

I refereed the game, had a couple of relaxing days on the beach with its beautiful white sand, chilled out, and then it was time to fly home again. Problem. World Rugby had again paid for a seat just for the trophy, but at the airport we were told the connecting flight back to Barbados was overbooked.

I told James, 'It looks like either me, you or this trophy is not getting on the plane.'

'Well, I'm not getting on the plane without the trophy,' he made it abundantly clear, fully aware of his responsibilities to bring it back home securely and in one piece.

I said, 'Well, I'll be getting on the plane without you and the trophy if necessary because I'm going home!'

Of course, I would have stayed and got on the next flight with James and the trophy, but I wasn't going to say that at the time! As it happens, we each managed to get through check-in and, more importantly, so did the Webb Ellis Cup, which once again took pride of place on the plane. I wonder if football's World Cup, or the UEFA Champions League trophy, has a fully-paid seat of its own, seat belt wrapped around securely, when it's taken to another country?

Two games later, still during that summer of 2016, was a landmark match for me. I took charge of my 71st international, and in doing so surpassed the appearances' record held by South Africa's Jonathan Kaplan, who had refereed at the top level over a 17-year period between 1996 and 2013. Again, it wasn't the most high-profile of fixtures, Fiji versus Tonga in the Pacific Nations Cup, but it meant everything to me, as you can imagine. I also knew there were still many more matches in me to come, so I would probably leave Kaplan's 70-cap mark, an incredible feat in itself, way behind by the time I'd finished. I'd also never refereed in any of the Pacific Islands previously, so I was looking forward to this one for many reasons.

That game was actually part of a hectic period which was to see me away from home for a whole month. It had begun in Edinburgh towards the end of May when I refereed Connacht versus Leinster in the PRO12 final at Murrayfield. It was a brilliant all-Irish affair, Connacht winning 20–10 to lift the trophy for the first time. The scenes were so jubilant afterwards, it was as if the whole of Galway had descended on the Scottish capital for the evening.

There was a touching moment when Leinster and Ireland scrum-half Eoin Reddan came into my changing room to see me. I'd refereed him from the beginning of his career with Connacht, then with Munster, Wasps, Leinster and the Irish national side, and always got on well with him. Eoin was a very underrated player by some, but I could see the huge part he played in the success of Wasps, Leinster and Ireland. He came in to give me his jersey and said, 'Nige, you've refereed me all my career and now I'm finished. So here, have this as a thank you for putting up with me as a player.' What a lovely gesture from a great guy and a wonderful rugby talent. He'd just lost the final, remember, yet took the trouble to do this. That jersey is now on display at Pontyberem RFC.

As for my own manic schedule, I couldn't even go home to Wales as I had to fly immediately to a four-day referees' camp in Cape Town, then on to Australia, before getting a connection to the Fijian capital of Suva for my record-breaking 71st match. I was then due to head back to Australia again to officiate in England's three-Test summer tour down under versus the Wallabies. But, the intensity of everything, the tight turnaround, caught up with my body, meaning I actually limped onto the plane heading to Cape Town because of a problem with my Achilles. It was touch-and-go whether I'd even be fit for my record-breaking match, but after some treatment by a South African doctor, a couple of injections and six days rest, I was able to start running again and was given the go-ahead for Fiji against Tonga.

I'd never been to Fiji before but if you do anything in rugby they will know who you are out there. They're absolutely fanatical about the game. People on the other side of the street were shouting out 'This is Not Soccer!' to me! They were so welcoming, and the trip was made even better when Anthony Buchanan, then chairman of the World Rugby referees' selection committee and a former Wales prop I knew quite well, flew out to present me with a silver plate with my name inscribed on it to mark the special occasion.

The game, won 23–18 by the Fijians, was uneventful, which was more than could be said for my next experience as I headed straight back to Australia. Firstly, I ran touch for Craig Joubert in the second Wallabies versus England Test in Melbourne, then I took charge of the third game myself in Sydney. Two strong rugby characters, Michael Cheika and Eddie Jones, were in charge of the teams, and let's just say they weren't exactly shy in coming forward with their views during that series, whether about each other, their teams or indeed the refereeing.

Jones had only recently become England coach, so there was bound to be a bit of extra spice given his first tour with the Red Rose was back in his native Australia. Of course, he'd taken the Wallabies to the World Cup final when they lost on home soil to Clive Woodward's England in 2003. So there was plenty of history and needle between these two teams. I suspected that Cheika and Jones, neither of whom wanted to take a backward step or appear weak, weren't going to be particularly quick to put out the flames.

England had won the first of three Tests 28–39 in Brisbane, but Cheika wasn't happy with the refereeing of Roman Poite, and that created a bit of extra tension heading into the next encounter seven days later.

Now, the day before a game the coaches are allowed to meet the referee to discuss any concerns they might have, particularly with the opposition. Normally, in a situation like this, you'd meet England, say at 3pm, then Australia two hours later, and go through everything you want and expect from the two sides. On this occasion the Wallabies invoked a clause which I didn't even know existed, entitling them to be present at the same time as England. In other words, the meeting was to be a joint one.

Craig Joubert seemed a bit nervous about this. I don't think he particularly likes confrontation, and the fact that Cheika and Jones had already been having spats with one another in the press during the build-up made matters worse. I told Craig, 'Look, just chair the meeting. See what they've each got to say. Act neutral, tell them what you think, and it'll be fine, I'm sure.' The meeting was indeed OK, but the following day England won again, this time convincingly by 7–23, and Cheika wasn't happy once more.

I was referee for the third Test, with England seeking an historic clean sweep and the Wallabies absolutely determined to not let that happen. By this stage we were coming towards the end of June. I'd been away from home for 28 days already since that PRO12 final at Murrayfield, and I was understandably a little weary with all the travelling. So when I arrived mid-afternoon from Melbourne at Sydney's Coogee Bay Hotel, a beautiful location right on the waterfront, I just wanted to unpack, get some shut-eye and a little of the tiredness out of my system, perhaps have a walk on the sand early evening to freshen up, then a bite to eat.

I drew the curtains, lay down on the bed and was out like a light pretty much the moment my head hit the pillow. I'd barely had ten minutes of sleep when the phone shrilled. It was Scott Young, Australia's referees' manager, on the other end of the line.

'I'm sorry to bother you Nigel, but we are going to have to move hotels.'

'What do you mean?' I replied. 'I've only just got here, unpacked and everything. You must be joking.'

Australia, apparently, weren't overly-happy that I was staying at the same hotel where England had also based themselves. It was a sheer coincidence that Rugby Australia had booked me into there, too.

'Well, can't you tell England to move?!' I said.

'Oh, I don't think we can ask them to do that,' Scott replied, not realising my comment had been rather tongue-in-cheek.

So I had to get up, pack my suitcase again, and was off on my travels once more, albeit this time just a few miles down the road to the Sydney Harbour Marriott Hotel, another lovely location on the seafront. Finally, the chance to relax. Not that it lasted.

Now, this was the week of the Brexit referendum vote. That took place on the Thursday back home and on the Friday out in Australia it was my turn to host the pre-match meeting with Cheika and Jones at 5pm. At the designated hour myself and my touch judges, Craig Joubert and New Zealand official Mike Fraser, walked into the room and we were quickly followed in by Eddie Jones, his forwards coach Steve Borthwick and England's team manager.

No sign of Australia.

Remember, we were ten hours ahead and news had only just started filtering through about the likely final outcome of the Brexit vote. We were chatting about that somewhat surprise outcome, explaining how we'd been having a coffee earlier with someone high up in the world of finance who'd told us what he thought was happening because he could see what the markets were doing.

Four minutes went by, five minutes, still no sign of Australia. More Brexit conversation, more about the financial markets, a bit more small-talk. Then, suddenly, Australia walked through the door – the team manager, forwards coach, and Stephen Larkham, their backs coach. No sign of Cheika.

The first thing Larkham said was to carry on with what was being discussed; they'd have their say afterwards.

I explained we weren't discussing rugby at all, we'd been talking about Brexit.

'We haven't started the meeting yet,' I told Larkham. At this point Eddie Jones turned to the Wallaby contingent and rapped, 'See, this is your problem mate. You've come in here ten minutes late, haven't even apologised to the referee for being late, and yet jump to conclusions when we haven't even started the meeting. We've been waiting for you.'

At that, he promptly got up, looked at me and said, 'I'm not putting up with this and neither should you Nigel. I'm sorry, but we're off mate.'

Refereeing France v Ireland in 2018, one of the most difficult games I've refereed. Johnny Sexton dropped a goal to win the game after a record 46 phases.

The opening game of the 2019 World Cup, Japan v Russia, with my two assistant referees, Matt Carley and Nic Berry.

Enjoying the 2019 Rugby World Cup semi-final between Wales v South Africa with Barrie.

Getting ready for the post-match black-tie dinner with my team of officials and good friends, Leighton Hodges, Pascal Gaüzère and TMO Simon McDowell.

My last ever Test match, with my assistant referees Mike Adamson and Matt Carley. My only regret is that I wish I had known it was my last. With a special French match jersey presented to me, with 'Nigel Owens 100th Test match' embroidered on it.

how it started

how it ended

Tests as referee: 100
Tests as assistant referee: 101
Tests as TMO: 9
Total Tests: 210
Four Rugby World Cups
Rugby World Cup final

As someone once put on Twitter, 'How it started and where it ended'.

Not the glamour of a Test match, but before the Young Farmers' Clubs' Sevens final at the Royal Welsh Show. A game that would last an hour and ten minutes, instead of the standard ten minutes each way!

A tribute dinner for me in Cardiff, where my good friends John Lacey, Wayne Barnes, Derek Bevan, Ed Morrison and Bob Yeman came along too.

A great honour to have the bar at Pontyberem RFC named after me. My good friends Jonathan 'Jiffy' Davies and Phil 'Tulip' Davies kindly opened the bar with me.

Always enjoyed refereeing local games in Wales.

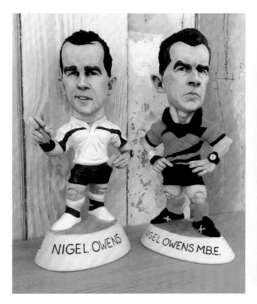

Two of the different Groggs that have been made of me.

The dream team. Filming for the *Jonathan* TV show with good friends Jonathan Davies and the lovely talented Sarra Elgan.

The things I do on the *Jonathan* programme!

Celebrating my surprise happy 50th birthday TV programme. With my dad, uncle Emrys, cousin Helen and her husband Gwyndaf, and their son Ifan. My cousin Mared was taking the photo, so couldn't be in it.

My father and uncle Emrys in the audience for my 50th birthday TV programme.

A day in the studio with a very good friend, the late Tommo.

The late, great Eddie Butler filming down on the farm during my first Six Nations after retiring. I was so shocked and saddened to hear of his passing. A great man.

A great honour to be accepted into the Gorsedd, with Non Evans who was being inducted the same day.

Receiving my honorary fellowship at the University of South Wales, with Phil Davies.

A good friend for many years, the Ferret, Jonathan Clayton.

A very rare holiday away during the season. Lanzarote, with my cousins Adrian, Wayne and Elis Nicholas.

My dad and his brother Emrys sitting on the seat the welfare committee in Mynyddcerrig very kindly placed at the bottom of the street in memory of my mother Mair and aunty Caerwen Owens.

With my godson Gwion at a family wedding many years ago.

My godson Efan, with a calf on his farm.

Enjoying a local night out with one of my good friends, Wayne Thomas. He scored that winning try when I missed the conversion in front of the posts – the time when my playing career ended and my refereeing one began.

A day out in New Quay, Ceredigion, with my godson Efan and his brothers Elis and Ioan.

Family and friends enjoying a pint in between filming, with Scott Quinnell at Mynyddcerrig club.

Having Christmas dinner with my dad two days before Christmas, as I had to fly out to referee Munster v Leinster on Boxing Day.

Me and Barrie with our stock bull, Dendor Sugar Ray. What a legend – the bull that is!

Feeding the Mairwen Herd. As you can see, Barrie isn't really dressed for it like me!

With my beloved girls, Bella and Aria, forever faithful and truly a man's best friend.

Me and Barrie with our litter of pups. All now gone to a good loving home.

On a pink tractor, raising money for breast cancer, with my cousin Dai Lewis and good friend Arwel, Cottage, and his son Gwion.

My father with uncle Emrys and Eiry … celebrating her 92nd birthday.

A day out walking, with my father, cousin Alan Rees and family friend Cecil Jones.

Christmas time with the out-laws ... oops, in-laws! Barrie's mum Linda, dad Eirwyn, twin brother Huw and his girlfriend Fflur.

Life at home. Me and Barrie looking forward to the future.

Borthwick had a big file open on his lap in front of him. He looked at me, then up at Eddie Jones, who by now was heading for the door. Borthwick closed his file and also made to leave.

Jones turned back to me and said, 'Look Nigel, you carry on with your meeting, but you shouldn't have to put up with this – and I certainly don't.'

I told him, 'Eddie, I'm going to have to hold the meeting, with or without you. It's the rules. Anything that comes up which is relevant to you, I'll speak to you about it in the changing room before the game tomorrow, or I can give you a call later if that works best?'

'That's fine mate, tomorrow is fine,' Eddie replied, and off they went.

Larkham looked a bit startled and, as I tried to start proceedings he asked, 'What are we doing? Are we waiting for them to come back?'

'Well I don't think they're going to be f*****g coming back, do you?'

Pre-match shenanigans, eh? Ironically, after all that, Australia and England served up a spellbinding game of rugby the following day. Jones' England team won a 40–44 thriller to make it a 3–0 clean sweep. We even had a rugby first of an up-and-under kick hitting one of those overhead cameras, with the ball completely changing direction as it came back down. I didn't know what to do, so I waved play on. Afterwards, a directive came which said in a situation like that a scrum should be awarded. We all knew from there on in, but I was certainly caught unawares at the time.

It was another of those classics. Bernard Foley, Dane Haylett-Petty, Michael Hooper and Israel Folau were among the try scorers for the Wallabies, who led at half-time, but still it wasn't enough as Billy Vunipola, Mike Brown, Dan Cole and Jamie George hit back for England and Owen Farrell was imperious with the boot as he kicked 24 points to secure victory in a see-saw thriller.

Eddie Jones and Michael Cheika should both have been proud of their teams. I guess these are two giants of the game who are just incredibly passionate men, wearing their rugby heart on their sleeve. I recall walking off the pitch after the World Cup final to see Cheika standing there, looking at me and shaking his head. I thought what the heck is he shaking his head at me for, his team have just been well beaten by the better side, there were no real controversies. But that's in his character, he doesn't like losing – which is the same with every great coach.

I then saw the other side of Cheika after I announced my Test retirement in 2020. He was the first leading figure in the game to send me an email, congratulating me on my career, on and off the field, and wishing me the best for my next chapter. It was a lovely email, and it meant a lot to me. Here was a guy who'd be banging your door down if his team had lost, be that Australia, Leinster or Stade Français, sometimes even if his side had won, yet he still took the time and trouble to do this for me.

Respect, Michael.

Which is more than I can say I had for Rod Kafer around that time, the former Australian fly-half/centre, who launched what I thought was a ridiculous attack on me when I took charge of another Wallabies defeat, their 37–10 Rugby Championship loss to old rivals New Zealand in Auckland four months after Sydney.

The controversy arose when I disallowed a try by Wallaby

wing Henry Speight, but Kafer was directing his ire at completely the wrong person. I'd been perfectly happy to award the score, but my TMO Shaun Veldsman came in to say a gold player, Dane Haylett-Petty, had impeded black, Julian Savea, in the build-up, thus supposedly stopping a try-saving tackle from being made.

Personally I felt it was a bit of a fifty-fifty, pulling and shoving on either side and that the TMO should not have come in on this occasion. But, once he decided to intervene, we had to be quite technical under the law in how we dealt with the issue. Shaun showed me footage on the big screen of Haylett-Petty pulling back Savea, but what he wasn't showing me was a similar grabbing from a New Zealand arm off the ball moments earlier.

I wasn't happy with this, but because all I could see was Haylett-Petty's offence, I had no option but to rule out the try. Well, you'd think World War III had broken out down under judging by some of the over-the-top reaction – this, remember, from a game the All Blacks had won more than comfortably, so that one incident hardly cost Australia the game.

Leading the charge was Kafer, capped 12 times by Australia, who said on his *Fox Sports* commentary, 'Nigel Owens should never referee a Test match again. That is disgraceful. He [Haylett-Petty] is behind the ball, he can run where he likes. It was a crucial decision that absolutely changed the course of this Test match.'

If I'd seen the whole footage, I'd have allowed the try. If the TMO had not come in, I'd have allowed the try. It was his intervention, coupled with the limited replays that they were showing me, that caused the complications. Whatever, though, it most certainly wasn't a decision that meant I 'should never referee a Test match again', as that clown said.

This wasn't going to put me off my stride. Indeed, the years 2016 and 2017 passed pretty quickly as I refereed more big Six Nations and Rugby Championship games, including a New Zealand 35–29 Australia rip-roarer in Dunedin, as well as a gripping 34–38 win for England in Argentina, and South Africa edging past France 17–18 in Paris. More classics. I still had the adrenaline and hype from the World Cup final, I was on something of a high … but I have to admit that I found 2018 really tough going. In many ways it was a make-or-break year for me – and it could easily have gone either way. Either you dig in and go to the 2019 World Cup still as one of the leading referees, or you say enough is enough, accept your heart is not really in it any more, and it's time to hang up the whistle. Momentarily, I faced that conundrum.

My real problem, I guess, was wondering what else did I really have to achieve? As well as the World Cup final, breaking Kaplan's Test record and overseeing some truly brilliant matches at the highest level, I'd just been chosen for three European Cup finals on the trot – Toulon's win over Clermont at Twickenham, Saracens beating Racing 92 the following year in Lyon, and Sarries once again in 2017, this time their glut of stars, including Owen Farrell, Maro Itoje and Billy Vunipola, overcoming Clermont at Murrayfield. What a game that was, a brilliant final, one of the most enjoyable of the seven I did.

The English and European champions really were a force to be reckoned with back then. Could Nigel Owens still be as a referee, or was he losing a little interest?

There were a couple of games early on in the year where

I found myself at the centre of controversy. The first was the Six Nations clash in Paris between France and Ireland when Johnny Sexton kicked a drop goal after about 40 phases of play right at the end to win the game 13–15 for the Irish. That was one of the toughest matches I have done. The contest at the breakdown was brutal at times and I got a bit of stick from Irish pundits and fans because I didn't produce a yellow card after Rob Kearney was tackled in the air.

It wasn't a yellow for me, just a penalty, that was easily enough explained. But when Ireland's coach Joe Schmidt questioned whether I had refereed the contact area strictly enough, I had to explain to him that you need to have an empathy for the game and sometimes let it flow. Joe likes a game to be refereed very technically, bordering on perfect, but that is impossible. As a rugby referee you can pretty much blow the whistle every single minute for one technical offence or another, but matches would be incredibly stop-start and indeed downright boring. Rugby would soon be in danger of becoming a turn-off for the paying customers or TV viewers. No-one would enjoy it.

One of the very reasons some of those classic matches I took charge of earned the rave reviews that they did was because of how they were 'managed'. You have to know when to blow the whistle, but, perhaps even more importantly, when not to, something which had been ingrained into me as a teenager taking my first tentative steps as a referee, as I've explained earlier in this book. The whistle was always held down by my side for a reason. There weren't too many grumbles about the breakdowns not being controlled strictly enough after those epic Tests I'd refereed, and trust me there were hugely physical collisions in every single one of them. South Africa versus New Zealand, England against France and also Australia, the Irish versus the All Blacks; Richie McCaw, Jerome Kaino and Kieran Read up against David Pocock and Michael Hooper in the World Cup final; no quarter asked and none given in any of those games, I can assure you. I pointed out to Joe Schmidt this was how I looked to referee matches; apply the law when there is something clearly wrong, certainly, but also be sensible about it on occasion. Get the big decisions right, but manage the match. I wasn't going to change my style of refereeing that had got me to the top and kept me there for over 15 years.

One month on from that bruising Stade de France encounter, I was in charge of another really difficult Irish–French encounter, a hugely competitive and combative Heineken Cup quarter-final between Munster and Toulon at a packed and vibrant Thomond Park, which the hosts just edged 20–19. There was an incident right at the beginning, the very first minute in fact, when Toulon wanted a penalty try as Chris Ashton chased a kick from his scrum-half Éric Escande, but was denied scoring as Munster's Simon Zebo raced across at full pelt to knock the ball dead with his hand.

My interpretation at the time was that it was a proper rugby challenge. Zebo tried to knock the ball away from Ashton, rather than deliberately and directly into touch, which would have been an offence, as Toulon clearly felt it was. The fact that the ball went into touch was an irrelevance to me, it was the action that mattered. I referred the matter upstairs, looked up at the big screen, carefully weighed up what I was seeing and told my touch judges Ian Davies and Ben Whitehouse, and my TMO Jonathan Mason, that

I thought it should be a scrum to Munster because Ashton had knocked-on first. I asked if anyone disagreed; they all agreed.

Shortly afterwards there was another decision, which again went in Munster's favour and caused further furore. Toulon had scrambled back to defend a through-kick by forming a ruck right by their own try line, but the ball was knocked-on at the base by their hooker Guilhem Guirado and the quick-thinking Lions scrum-half Conor Murray came round, picked it up and calmly touched down over the line. It went to the TMO again. We took way too long to make the decision because the wrong pictures were being shown. Eventually, after what seemed an eternity out there, with me looking at my watch a couple of times to express my dissatisfaction, the correct angle showed Guirado had definitely knocked-on, as I'd suspected, meaning the ruck was over. Clearly knowing the laws, the alert Murray was entitled to come round and get the ball, as I explained to Toulon's captain Mathieu Bastareaud, but the French side were very unhappy.

I'm always open to accepting when I've got something wrong. We all make mistakes and I'm no different to anybody else in that respect. Thus, when I reviewed the game afterwards I accepted that I had erred on the first incident and should indeed have given a penalty try against Zebo, but I had called the complicated Murray incident correctly. So it wasn't too bad really, I guess, considering how much had been going on during a frenetic 80 minutes of pulsating, non-stop, truly combative rugby.

Imagine my shock then when I read a critical column the former England and Lions star-turned-pundit Austin Healey penned for the *Daily Telegraph* five days later. It was headlined 'Is Nigel Owens now too much of a celebrity to referee the big games?' He wrote that I was supposedly refereeing to the sound of my own whistle, even suggested I might be moulding the laws to my own wishes. For good measure, Austin threw in the fact that I had my own talk show on Welsh TV channel S4C, and a column for the national newspaper of Wales, the *Western Mail*, where he'd noted I'd just discussed Brexit. He went on to write, 'I can't think of a referee in any sport who has built up a profile like his and being able to pull it off.'

I studied Austin's words from start to finish and, as well as providing an element of disbelief on my part, his column also got me thinking. I asked myself whether I thought Austin had a point? No, he hadn't, I concluded. I may not have been refereeing as well as I should have, not to the high standards I set myself anyway. I accepted that. But it had absolutely nothing to do with my off-the-field activities, or liking the sound of my own whistle, or anything remotely like that. I was doing TV work, or stand-up comedy, way before I took up professional refereeing, so it certainly wasn't a case that I needed the sport's platform to become a celebrity. I didn't want to be a celebrity, didn't view myself as one, either.

I wondered if Healey was still not happy after a Dragons versus Leicester match at Rodney Parade in the old Anglo-Welsh Cup where I'd awarded a scrum to the Welsh side. Healey, in my view trying to be clever, shouted out, 'Whose ball is it ref?'

I replied, 'It's ours,' as a joke. He didn't appear to be amused.

Whatever Healey wrote these many years on, I knew the bigger issue was that 2018 was just one of those in-between years for me. In the back of my mind I was thinking about whether I really wanted to go to Japan for the World Cup, spend eight weeks on the other side of the planet, away from home, my friends and family. This, coupled with having already achieved pretty much everything in the game, created something of a double-whammy effect. As such, complacency had clearly set in. I'd lost a bit of interest during that period.

So my view was that Healey was right in one sense, I didn't referee that Munster versus Toulon game particularly well. But he was wrong in another sense, in that it had nothing to do with celebrity status or the other arguments he was putting forward. My poor form was down to my own mindset and how difficult that particular year was for someone who had already refereed all the big games.

That week served as something of a watershed moment. I sat down and thought to myself, I'm not going to give Healey, that Kafer bloke, or anybody else for that matter, any more ammunition to throw at me. In other words, it was make your mind up time Nigel. Do you really want to carry on refereeing like this if your heart isn't really in it any more, or are you going to say, right, time to get back to the standards you set yourself? And maintain them, too.

The choice was mine and it was as binary as that. That was when I decided I definitely wanted to go through to the 2019 World Cup. It was time to knuckle down, work hard and be the referee I knew I could be again, but wasn't at that particular point of my career.

I couldn't do this on my own, though. I spoke to Paul Adams, the WRU's newly-appointed referees' chief, who had taken over from Nigel Whitehouse, and explained to him that now Derek Bevan had finished his rugby duties, not just as a TMO but also as my coach after the World Cup final, I was beginning to notice a bit of a problem. Other than Paul himself and Joël Jutge, I felt I was finding it very difficult for people to be honest with me, mainly I guess because of what I'd achieved in the game. If I made up my mind on a decision during a match, I felt that the other officials would tend to agree with me instead of challenging it. I believed there were quite a few examples of that.

I always encouraged my fellow officials to speak up if they believed I'd got something wrong, even if it was as simple as, 'Hang on a moment, Nigel. You might want to look at that again.' International rugby today is played at such a frantic pace. With so much going on, it's impossible for the referee to see everything. You most definitely need to work as a team. That wasn't always happening in the way I was of the opinion it should do.

Maybe some just weren't good enough to challenge me. Maybe others thought we can't possibly question Nigel, he's the best in the world. Yes, you can. I'm not perfect, so let me know where you feel I might have gone wrong. If after another look we find I was correct all along, so be it. No problem.

Part of me felt, rightly or wrongly, that there may even have been a tiny handful who wanted me to get things wrong. I've been at refereeing camps where I've heard comments like, 'Did you see so-and-so reffing at the weekend? He had a bad game.' Hang on now fellows, I'd say we're all in this together. My view was if someone wanted to climb the ladder, or get the big games, then do that with your own ability, rather than mocking someone for failing.

Whatever, it was obvious I badly needed another set of eyes to analyse my performances. Paul Adams was very understanding about my predicament, indeed he was always very supportive. So we agreed to approach David McHugh, the former top Irish referee who had just resigned from a senior management role with the Irish Rugby Football Union and whose strength was, in actual fact, coaching. I knew David well, having been his touch judge in the Six Nations when first breaking through myself. So we met for a coffee all these years on, and I asked if he would like to coach me.

David said he'd be delighted to. There and then we agreed on a goal – to go through to the World Cup the following year and make it very, very difficult for them not to pick me for the final again. We set the bar high deliberately. From here on in, Austin Healey and the other critics were going to find very little to question about me in newspaper columns.

David started his work with me in the summer of 2018 and my first game was a pre-season affair between Bristol and the Scarlets. It wasn't a competitive match, a friendly played over four 20-minute periods, and I just let things go. Way too much in fact, as David spelt out in no uncertain terms afterwards. He phoned to say, 'This is actually a good start … because I don't want to see you refereeing like that again!'

It was the early pull your socks up message I needed from him. David continued, 'If you started off at the level you are capable of, it would be very difficult for me to say anything constructive for improvement. But this gives me a few things to work on with you.'

Those things included a few positional changes on the field. David noticed that I was running into places I shouldn't be. He explained how I needed to conserve my energy more as I was getting older. His advice enabled me to be sharper around the breakdown and return to the standards I had set myself previously. The little things David spotted, his guidance and extra eyes, meant I was able to go to the World Cup in Japan 12 months later in top form once more. Indeed, he actually coached me right through to the end of my Test career. I'm pretty sure I wouldn't have been at the height of my game were it not for his support. Just like Derek Bevan previously, David McHugh coached me on and off the field with his excellent words of wisdom.

There was a bit of a shock just before the World Cup started as myself and England's top official Wayne Barnes weren't given a single Rugby Championship fixture in the summer of 2019. That disappointed me as it would almost certainly have been my last opportunity to go to New Zealand, Australia or South Africa to referee, places where I had always received a wonderful welcome and where the rugby was so intense.

By now, the Irish official Alain Rolland had taken over from Joël Jutge as World Rugby's High Performance Match Officials' Manager and, although he didn't tell me this himself, he explained to Paul Adams that the plan was for the powers-that-be to look after myself and Barnsey as two of the more experienced officials, to cut down on our travelling ahead of Japan, and enable us to go into the World Cup completely fresh.

'Well that doesn't make sense,' I told Paul, pointing out how World Rugby instead had me heading out to Fiji to referee two games in the Pacific Nations Cup, USA v Samoa and Tonga v Canada. In fact, it was part of a crazy itinerary that also saw me fly to Japan for a three-day referees' camp – a team-bonding exercise we didn't really need – and also take charge of two World Cup warm-up friendlies between France and Scotland, then England versus Ireland, with Eddie Jones' men winning that one 57–15. The margin of victory was a bit of a shock, given Ireland had been the best team in the world, but it certainly put down a World Cup marker for England. I was looking forward to seeing and refereeing them at the upcoming tournament.

Shortly before heading home from the referees' camp we were handed our 2019 World Cup appointments, so we knew them well in advance. I was given the opening game between hosts Japan and Russia, not Tier 1 nations but a huge honour, of course, plus two other smaller matches – Italy versus Canada and USA against Tonga – and thus only England versus Argentina as what you would class a big game in the group stages. Joël Jutge may have stood down from the top position, but he was still very much involved in the decision-making process as part of the referees' selection committee, and he surprised me a little by saying, 'You're not our priority, Nigel. We know what you can do. We need to prioritise the other referees.'

I replied, 'Whoa Joël, your priority should be to appoint the best referees to the big games, not just appoint others and hope they'll do well. The first thing you need to do is respect the game with the correct appointments. Do that and everybody who proves up to the task gets a chance to do the final.'

Back home in Wales, taking stock of all this ahead of the tournament before flying back out to Japan again, I realised Joël's words meant that I was very much on the back foot. I just had a nagging feeling some of them didn't really want to pick me, probably because I'd already done everything. If anything, this actually further stiffened my resolve to go out there and make it hard for them not to select me for the final, whether I'd done it once or not. If they reckoned I was going to make things easy for them, they had another think coming!

The opening match was set for 20 September in Tokyo between Japan and Russia. I was really looking forward to it, but almost didn't make it. Two days before I was due to head to the Far East, I refereed Cardiff versus Pontypridd in the Welsh Premiership. One of the players swung round in the tackle and caught me on the calf with his leg. It was really painful, I could barely walk, and needed treatment from the club physios. I had wonderful support from Pat Moran at the WRU, the Cardiff Blues team doctor and my local GP Dr Gareth. I went for an MRI scan in hospital. It was touch-and-go, but thankfully the scan revealed there was no tear, just bruising. Whilst we put my flight back by a few days, eventually I was able to get on a plane and prove my fitness once out in Tokyo. Little did I know it at the time, but the calf was to cause me issues again just before the final.

We'll come to that in a moment. First things first – Japan versus Russia. What an occasion! A sell-out crowd, the Emperor of Japan and other dignitaries present, Vladimir Putin had been invited, the eyes of the world were on us. Bizarre then that within the confines of the dressing room, just before kick-off, two people in one corner were speaking to each other in Welsh as we discussed what was ahead – myself and Russia's coach Lyn Jones. I knew Lyn well from his time with the Ospreys and Neath previously. I wonder what language Lyn's Russian players thought we were conversing in, let alone what we were saying to one another!

As it was the opening game, the onus was on me, of course, to set the barometer for refereeing standards at the tournament. The hosts won 30–10 and I received a report of 'very good' – which was later downgraded to 'good' because I hadn't penalised or given a yellow card to one of the Russian players for a late tackle, something I didn't see because my back was turned and my eyes were in the direction of the ball, as should be the case. The TMO did spot the incident, but for whatever reason he didn't bring it to my attention and was happy, in his view, that it didn't warrant a sanction.

I told my assessors that if I'd seen what happened in the first place then fair enough, but they can't downgrade me because of the failure of the TMO to act as he should have done. During the tournament they changed their approach on this, but my review from the opening game still only stayed as 'good', much to my annoyance I can tell you. The buck stops with you as the referee, and rightly so, but you can't be held responsible for something that is humanly impossible for you to see and which should be a non-negotiable decision for the TMO.

As the tournament progressed, there was a bit of unrest behind the scenes at the way feedback was being given. One or two referees were getting 'very good', yet when we analysed their performances we all knew it clearly wasn't of that standard. Conversely, World Rugby also went public in saying that the officiating as a whole after the first couple of rounds was not good enough; there weren't enough red cards being brandished to crack down on foul play.

This caused further disquiet, and you could see that a lot of the referees were feeling under pressure, clearly not enjoying the games and it affected their performances.

Maybe it was simply down to my experience, and dare I say it belief in my own ability to cope with anything, but I was enjoying the World Cup and received excellent feedback from my other three group matches: Italy 48–7 Canada, USA 19–31 Tonga, and England 39–10 Argentina. In that last game I had to send off the Pumas' second-row Tomás Lavanini early on because of a reckless tackle, when his shoulder made contact with Owen Farrell's jaw. England, clearly the better team anyway, ran away with the game after this and I could sense one or two of the Argentine players wanted to blame me for what was happening. At the end of the match their captain, Pablo Matera, as well as their ex-skipper and hooker Agustín Creevy, refused to shake my hand, and Matera just gave me an evil glare with his eyes. I think that's the only time this has happened to me. I felt disappointed because the values of our game are so much better and bigger than that. In that moment Matera certainly made me feel he wasn't the kind of person you'd want to cross. Yet, the truth is, it was a blatant sending-off offence. Lavanini's challenge on Farrell was reckless. I took decisive action even though we were early into the game and I received an excellent review from my World Rugby assessors.

It all meant that, come the knockout stages, despite the talk of younger referees being prioritised and developed, we were down to the same old stagers once more – Wayne Barnes, Jaco Peyper of South Africa, the Frenchman Jérôme Garcès and myself.

I was given the Ireland versus New Zealand quarter-final in Tokyo, which was a seismic clash of two top teams. Many had predicted beforehand that any meeting between these two countries would happen in the final itself, given the pedigree of the All Blacks and the fact that the Irish had been number one in the world rankings the previous year, beating New Zealand twice in their last three meetings. As it happened, it proved to be a one-sided affair, the All Blacks running out comfortable 46–14 victors. As for me, well things were going exactly to plan and I received another 'excellent' report from my assessor, putting me in line for the semi-finals. I obviously couldn't do Wales versus South Africa, so they gave me New Zealand against England in Yokohama – the biggest game of the tournament, two great rugby nations who had only met once in the previous five years, and two massive coaches coming together to lock horns in Steve Hansen and Eddie Jones.

It was the best game of the World Cup, played at incredible speed, with thrilling rugby and intensity produced by both sides. I just sensed something special was about to unfold when England formed a V-shape to stare down the Haka before kick-off. It was a spine-tingling moment, and standing in the middle of it I could sense the passion on both sides, and I knew I needed to keep an eye on it in case it turned ugly. Thankfully, it didn't. England made their point but were respectful in doing so.

Some of the English players had crossed the halfway line, but this is not actually allowed. As such, I had to quietly give a nod to their scrum-half Ben Youngs, a great player and person that I have the utmost respect for, pointing out he needed to get back. He duly did so. Opposite me on the other side of the V was prop Joe Marler, a really colourful character in our game. I caught his eye too, nodded and discreetly pointed for him also to go back a few yards. Typical Marler, he stuck his tongue out at me! I giggled to myself and thought, well stay there then if you're going to!

This response to the Haka proved to be the precursor to an epic 80 minutes of rugby. The two sides went absolutely hammer and tongs at each another. England stormed into a 10–0 lead after a Manu Tuilagi try in only the second minute, and were only denied the chance to extend that by brilliant defence from the reigning champions, who certainly weren't giving up their crown without a fight. New Zealand came back hard, but England's own defence held firm and the goalkicking excellence of George Ford and Owen Farrell meant they emerged 19–7 victors. England really were on top form that day; they also had two tries disallowed – correctly so, I must stress!

The All Blacks had not lost a World Cup game in 12 years but, as the BBC put it, 'England tore the crown from their head with a performance of unremitting energy and excellence on a night for the ages in Yokohama.' It was certainly a huge privilege to be in the centre of it all, to marvel close-up at some of the rugby played, indeed wince at the ferocity of much of the tackling from the likes of Maro Itoje, Tom Curry, Courtney Lawes, Brodie Retallick, Ardie Savea and Keiran Read. But here's a little secret for you. Just 25 minutes into the game I felt my calf go again and needed treatment in the dressing room at half-time. The medics managed to patch me up, but I refereed the rest of that semi-final, this thrilling end-to-end affair played at real tempo throughout, at no more than 60 per cent capacity. I needed to use every single ounce of the experience I'd accrued down the years to know precisely where to run, when I had to run, and absolutely no more than that. The positional training David McHugh had given me the previous summer was certainly paying off.

The calf got really painful around the 60-minute mark,

but no way was I leaving that field. Adrenaline helped get me through. Top-class rugby is played at such an incredible pace and, I guess, refereeing six matches at the World Cup, plus three as touch judge, in a short period of five weeks, took its toll on an ageing body like mine.

Joël Jutge told me afterwards the reason I could referee the England v New Zealand semi-final so well, when clearly not fit, was because, 'You could see the players had respect for you and knew exactly what you wanted from them.'

There was another lovely moment when my TMO Marius Jonker presented me with a match ball the rival captains Owen Farrell and Kieran Read had signed. They wrote 'Best wishes Nige', a lovely gesture from two men who are an absolute credit to the sport, great players and excellent captains. They sensed it would be my last World Cup game, hence the tribute, but would it be? What chance of back-to-back finals for me?

On this occasion, unlike in 2015 when I was given news of my final appointment before the semis, World Rugby held off naming the referee until they knew which two teams would be involved. As it was, South Africa joined England in reaching the final by narrowly overcoming Warren Gatland's Wales in the second Yokohama semi-final. Technically, given that Wales were out, it meant I was still in with a shout.

The top English referee Wayne Barnes had been pencilled in for the final, but he was now out of the equation for obvious reasons. So too was the South African Jaco Peyper, although he had blotted his own copybook anyway after posing for that photograph with Welsh fans simulating the elbow action of a French player he'd red carded against Gatland's side in their last-eight showdown.

Because I'd just received another glowing report from Joël and his colleagues, suddenly it seemed to boil down to a straight choice between two people – the Frenchman Jérôme Garcès, or me again, albeit he was very much the favourite now I must stress. Jérôme and myself were in the last few games of our careers, but certainly he had been refereeing well enough to do the final. He was a quality official, make no mistake about that. The trouble was that, like me, he was also injured and, as such, the announcement had to be delayed longer than World Rugby had anticipated.

Deep down, sadly, I knew I wasn't going to be fit. That damn calf I'd injured back home in Wales just before flying out for the tournament had flared up again and, perhaps making sure I finished that England win over New Zealand, whilst injured, made it a touch worse. The day after my own semi-final I went to watch the other one between Wales and South Africa. A group of us caught a train to the ground, and what should have been a 20-minute walk from the station to the stadium took more like an hour and 20 minutes by the end, for a number of reasons. Firstly, I couldn't walk properly, thus had to go very slowly. Secondly, people wanted to stop for photos or a chat.

'Great performance yesterday, Nige,' some would say. 'Why are you limping, Nige?' others would ask. And limping I most certainly was. That walk was quite painful, believe me, and I ended up having to drag one foot behind the other. But I'm always happy to stop and talk. I guess that gave me momentary respite from the pain. This camaraderie is what helps make our sport so special and I would never wish to be aloof or anything like that. So, if the journey to our seats inside the ground took more time than it should have done, so be it.

Joël Jutge told me he said to his fellow selectors, 'Nigel has made it very difficult for us not to give him the final again.' I'm informed there was a split vote on the decision. Some went for me, the majority for Garcès.

'What do you expect, Joël?' I fired back. 'I haven't come out here just to make up the numbers. But I feel some of the selectors have been looking at reasons not to appoint me, my age, the fact I've done the final before, the wish to develop new referees, rather than encourage myself and others to carry on while we're still at the top of our game. We should be backed – and the newcomers forced to come up to our level if you want them to get better.'

Look, I'm all for development, giving newbies an opportunity to prove their worth, but the balance has to be right. You don't throw away experience and know-how as readily as that. Whether you're 55 or 18, if you're up there as one of the best, don't just cast that aside for the wrong reasons.

I had to go into this tournament determined not to give them any excuse not to pick me, which is disappointing. But my stance was vindicated because I was down to the final two. As it happens, after it started to become clear my calf wasn't going to improve in time, I told them I wouldn't be able to do the final, and that Garcés should be getting it anyway. Whether he was fit or not, he deserved it and had been refereeing well. Yes, it was easy for me to say that because I was injured, but I honestly feel my principles and moral compass are such that I'd have been telling them that anyway even if fully fit.

I'd done the final once. It only comes around every four

years and this time they should give it to Jérôme. I knew from first-hand experience what an honour it was, what it would mean to him, and I was delighted for Jérôme when his family flew out for the game. He was extremely proud, just as I had been four years earlier at Twickenham.

My aim heading to Japan 2019 was to do a World Cup semi-final for the first time – and set the cat amongst the pigeons by making it difficult for them not to consider me for the final itself, too. I had achieved that. Mission accomplished. The next step, at the age of 48, was to consider how much longer I wished to continue refereeing, if at all?

Just as importantly, given what I felt was the World Rugby selectors' slightly negative stance towards me during the World Cup, what support would I actually get from them if I chose to carry on? Their chairman Anthony Buchanan had been so supportive of me during his tenure, whilst also being fair and honest in his views and choices, but he was now standing down. What might that mean for me with the rest of the selectors?

CHAPTER TEN

100 and out, but not quite the farewell planned

HAVING PRETTY MUCH achieved everything as a referee, I couldn't really ask for anything more in my career as I contemplated the next step after Japan. Well, proud Welshman that I am, in an ideal world I guess refereeing Wales in front of a huge crowd at the magnificent Principality Stadium would have been on my bucket list – but that wasn't going to happen, was it?

Wrong, Nigel. Wrong.

Within a matter of days after arriving home, batteries a little, if not fully recharged, I was afforded the rather surreal, but truly fabulous experience of standing out in the middle of the best rugby ground in the world, Wales team to my left, opposition to the right, singing the Welsh national anthem, 'Hen Wlad Fy Nhadau'.

Just one month after I'd done that brilliant England versus New Zealand semi-final in Yokohama, the Welsh Rugby Union had asked World Rugby if I could take charge of their November game in Cardiff against the Barbarians, Wales' first post the 11-year Warren Gatland era. It was a highly unusual request. You simply don't get to referee your own country, the side you naturally follow. So the positive reply received possibly came as something of a surprise to one or two.

Nigel Owens, who bleeds Welsh through and through, was to be the man in the middle for an international fixture involving the Wales national side in Cardiff. Welsh bias from me then? Not a bit of it. None whatsoever. What that game proved is what I've always known, that when I'm out there as a referee I'm completely neutral. I do my job fairly to the two teams and thus show respect to the game of rugby. Yes, I sang the national anthem along with the Wales players, loud and proud, too, but after that it was simply red versus black for 80 minutes as far as I was concerned. In front of nearly 63,000 passionate Welsh fans, it proved to be another memorable experience that I will always bank away in the memory, one I will never forget because of the unique nature of the occasion.

The natural assumption for Barbarians matches is that they are easy to referee, free-flowing, lots of tries, played in the right spirit – you just let the game flow. The opposite can often be true, though. They are quite awkward fixtures to handle in other ways, and having refereed four of them, Baa-Baas versus England twice, once against New Zealand and now Wales, I speak from first-hand experience.

Up-and-coming officials used to be appointed to these matches, a gentle first step on the international ladder, so to speak, before being handed the more rigorous challenge of a proper competitive Test. However, it quickly became something of a problem fixture because you would either let too much go, in typical Barbarians spirit, or blow the whistle too often, which simply ends up frustrating everybody. Striking the right balance isn't easy.

With all due respect, most of the Barbarians players are there to enjoy themselves. They don't care too much about scrums going down, or breakdown offences. But they are playing against a proper international team, and the laws still need to be applied, and there are times when you simply have to say enough is enough and penalise.

The younger officials sometimes failed to come to terms with these complexities, thus we started to see more experienced referees being appointed. As I say, this was my fourth time and it proved to be a wonderful homecoming from Japan. My partner Barrie came to watch. My dad, uncle Emrys and other members of the family also attended. That was lovely for me. Because the internationals I refereed were often in far-flung places, my family couldn't see lots of them in person. But they certainly enjoyed this one much closer to home – during and after the match, I might add.

I was staying at the Hilton Cardiff, a beautiful four-star hotel right opposite the castle in Cardiff's city centre and a stone's throw from the ground. The plan was for dad and uncle Emrys to meet my cousin Helen and her husband Gwyndaf at the Marriott Hotel afterwards, in a different part of the city centre, and then come along to the Hilton for a post-match celebration drink with me. They'd planned just one pint at the Marriott, but some Welsh fans from the Valleys were sitting nearby, realised that this was Nigel Owens' dad, got chatting away, bought him and uncle Emrys a drink; then another, then another. One and a half hours later they finally turned up in a, shall we say, rather bad way, to find me at the Hilton!

We had a great evening, myself, my family, my mentors David McHugh and Derek Bevan, my boss Paul Adams. A right old laugh. Indeed dad and uncle Emrys told us it was one of the most enjoyable nights they'd ever had – and that was probably nothing to do with the unique chance to watch me referee Wales in Cardiff, more that they had free beer all evening!

Earlier on, out on the field, a huge roar had erupted when Warren Gatland's face appeared on the big screen. He had coached Wales from 2008 through to October 2019, but this time he was sitting in the stands watching his former players, having stood aside to take up a new role in New Zealand. I also received plaudits when I left the field at the end, the Welsh players shaking my hand, saying they felt privileged to have me as referee in an international fixture, and there were some nice cheers from the fans.

That meant an awful lot of course, but the highlight of the day for me wasn't that moment. It came earlier on when Rory Best, the former Ireland captain and front-row warrior who was retiring from rugby, was substituted by the Baa-Baas midway through the second half. As Rory started to leave the pitch, the entire stadium, all four stands, rose to give him a standing ovation. I just thought to myself at the time, Wow, this is why we are so lucky to have the best supporters in the world in Wales. So passionate, so supportive of their own side, so full of belief, but also fair and appreciative of the opposition. This was not a Wales icon they were applauding, remember. This was someone who'd locked horns with their own team over the best part of a decade, one of the 'enemy'. Wales v Ireland had become a big rivalry, yet Rory received not just a gentle clap, but a huge roar.

It was a touching couple of minutes. I could see the emotion in Rory as he started to walk past me. 'Congratulations on a wonderful career,' I told him as he slowly made his way off. Rory is one of the good guys, a hugely respectful captain of Ireland and Ulster, a British Lion and someone for whom I have enormous regard.

He clearly felt the same way as I did about the Welsh support after what happened that day. I spoke to him afterwards about the reception he'd just received and he was genuinely taken aback by it, didn't expect that at all, and felt it was a brilliant way to bow out of rugby.

'That's the Welsh fans for you,' I told him. Rory had to agree.

For the record, Wales won 43–33. There were no complaints from either side and, another milestone chalked off, it was time to start looking ahead. What did the future hold for me now?

After every World Cup, when we've all had a little time to reflect and take stock, the World Rugby Match Officials' Manager, in effect the main man, and his fellow selectors sit down with you to analyse your performances, give feedback and assess where they see you going from there. If not exactly a one-to-one, you get the idea.

In 2007, my first tournament, the New Zealander Paddy O'Brien was the man in charge. He told me I'd done really well and, as such, I was definitely in contention to do the big games four years hence. Myself and Wayne Barnes had been shock selections for that World Cup, a few senior referees missed out as a result of these two newcomers on the block unexpectedly breaking through. There was no pressure on me, I didn't expect to do knockout games, but Paddy told me I'd been very much in the discussion for those. The future looked bright. I left that meeting on cloud nine, full of confidence.

I didn't go into the 2011 tournament in New Zealand in the best of form. I had those personal relationship break-up issues I've already discussed in a previous chapter, and it affected me during matches in the build-up. Paddy rang Bob Yeman, who was in charge of referees at the WRU, to tell him that, the way I was refereeing, I'd be lucky to go at all. In the end I did get selected, worked hard on my fitness, and blew it out of the park with my performances. At my post-tournament meeting, Paddy told me I'd done so well. My aim had to be a semi, or even the final itself, in 2015.

Again, I walked out of the room on a high, full of confidence, delighted with the feedback and support I was receiving.

Roll on a further four years to 2015 and I guess your debrief is very different when you've been chosen for the World Cup final. What are your plans Nigel? 'Well, I'm considered to be your number one referee, and I want to continue to be your best referee, go through to 2019 in Japan.'

That sounds good, they said. Once again I left with a big smile on my face. We were in harmony.

So, having just received excellent reviews for the vast majority of my six matches at the 2019 World Cup, and refereed perhaps the game of the tournament in England versus New Zealand, I'd hoped for similar positive noises once more when the time came for my post-tournament debrief. Unfortunately, it proved to be a little more complicated than that.

The four men sitting in judgement were Alain Rolland, who had taken over as referees' manager; Joël Jutge, his predecessor in the top role and now a selector; New Zealand's Lyndon Bray, and Wayne Erickson, the ex-Australian referee turned performance reviewer. They told me I had refereed brilliantly again and, as per normal, once more asked what my next ambitions were. What were my plans?

The truth is, this time I'd found it hard being away from home for almost eight weeks in Japan. At this stage I wasn't sure if I wanted to do that again in 2023, when the World Cup would be played in France. OK, that's only a short hop across the Channel compared to being out in the Far East, but it's still a big commitment. Remember, it's not just the tournament itself, but the time spent away in the build-up, refereeing matches on the other side of the world, or taking part in various referees' camps for days on end.

So I was honest with them.

'Look, I'm 48 years of age. You're basically asking me if I'm going to go through to 2023. I can't answer that,' I replied, explaining that I didn't know for certain what my ambition, or indeed my body, would be like in a few years time.

'All I ask is that you pick me on merit. So if my performances prove I'm still one of your best referees, I hope you'll continue to pick me next season and the season after. And let's see how it goes after that.'

Their response somewhat surprised and, I have to say, disappointed me a little. They couldn't do that, they explained. They needed to plan for 2023 and, in effect, required an answer from me there and then.

'Well, you're asking me a question I can't answer at the moment,' I repeated to the group. 'I think I've still got a huge amount to offer, on and off the field, and you need to take that into account, I'd suggest?'

Part of that, I emphasised, was being keen to support the younger referees coming through. I was more than happy to run touch for them, offer my experience, before, during and after matches, including how to deal with coaches and players, in order to help them make the necessary step-up that World Rugby wanted from them.

That would be a problem, I was told. Why? Because people, supposedly, would be asking why I wasn't refereeing the matches myself.

'Perhaps that's a question you should be asking yourselves then,' I responded. 'If I'm still one of your top referees, why not just let me carry on for another couple of years and then we'll see where we are at that point?' I reiterated.

I'd always got on well with Alain and Joël, in particular. It was a good, open and honest debate. We were all being frank with each another.

As it happens, I'd already been given France versus England in the Six Nations in February 2020, my 98th Test match, which meant I was only two games away from the century mark. The suggestion was that, like Richie McCaw and some other greats of the game, I could bow out at the very top. It would be a good way to go.

'Well, I'm confident I will be at the top of my game for a few years still, so now is not the right time to go at all. You're asking me to do something which doesn't feel right just yet,' I argued.

My view was that New Zealand wouldn't suddenly say to their best player, be that Richie McCaw, Dan Carter, Kieran Read or whoever, we're going to stop picking you just to give others a chance, when they themselves still had lots to offer as the old guard. No coach in the world would do that and I didn't really see why it should apply to referees, either.

Was it that they were now deciding on age, I wondered to myself? Wayne Barnes was told he would be OK to go on for another four years. We'd both started at the same time and had done four World Cups. So it must be coming down to age then, I felt. The Frenchman Romain Poite, a couple of years younger than me, was also told he was OK to carry on.

'What happens if I referee France against England really well? Why would you want me to finish?' I continued.

They knew I'd referee that game well, came the response. They couldn't really give me a proper answer, other than to say they needed to develop other younger referees. I certainly understood the need for that. It was a fair point, but I'd made it clear I too was prepared to help out as part of that plan. The conversation went on a bit, we were going round the houses somewhat, couldn't come to an agreement. So Alain Rolland brought the meeting to a close by saying that he and I should have a chat again after the Six Nations had finished in the spring. I suppose I was digging my heels in a bit now, as I felt they were telling me to finish on my own terms, yet were telling me when to finish!

Unlike those three previous post-World Cup debriefs, this time I felt a little bit deflated as I walked out of the door. I fully accepted the importance of development – we all have to start somewhere, I did myself back in the day – but you still have a duty to the actual game itself. That means picking the best referees to officiate the best games. When the opportunity then presents itself within that structure, development can be a part of that, but it should not be the be-all and end-all.

Other referees were telling me I could easily get to the next World Cup and that they wanted me to, but I wasn't quite so sure in my own mind. Before going to Japan, I'd bought cattle for my new farm which were to arrive around the time I was due to return. I was really excited about this and, coupled with missing my partner Barrie and my family, spending almost two months out in the Far East meant I was counting the days to get home towards the end.

Barrie is a teacher and had half-term off, but they kindly gave him another week's holiday on top so that he was able to fly out to be with me during the knockout stages. That made things more enjoyable. Perhaps it's one of the reasons why I refereed so well in the quarter-finals and semi-finals, but in truth by the end I couldn't wait to get home.

Did I really want to do that all over again in France? Did I really want to be on the other side of the world for weeks on end, at referees' camps, or doing New Zealand or Australia matches down under, if my dad possibly wasn't well? Did I really want to be away from Barrie for any length of time any more? My dad was now 85 years of age and, although in very good health, I wanted to be at home more to spend time with him, too.

Deep down, these were questions I'd started to ask myself anyway. But the fact that I wasn't exactly being overly encouraged at that post-tournament debrief also played on my mind. If, at that meeting, they'd said, Nigel, you're still a top referee and we definitely want you as part of the team for 2023, I'd have been left with a decision to make. Either knuckle down and look after your body, which I know I'd have been able to do, in order to carry on for another four years – or call it a day.

It wouldn't have been an easy choice, but I felt that choice was being taken away from me a little anyway. It was a strange feeling, because I'd become accustomed to such wonderful support and wholehearted backing from the World Rugby powers-that-be down the years.

Two things happened which changed the landscape further. The first was the coronavirus, and we all know how that altered everything. The other was Alain Rolland moving on from his top job in charge of us all and Paddy O'Brien taking over again on an interim basis whilst World Rugby advertised the role.

When Paddy phoned after the conclusion of the 2020 Six Nations – in effect the conversation I'd agreed to have with Alain – I told him I'd made up my mind. I wasn't going to hang around if they didn't really want me to any more. But, I was only two games away from 100 Tests and, although I'm not in rugby to reach any numbers, that clearly would be a very special milestone. I was also given good advice by the people I trusted. You will regret it if you don't fight to do the 100, they said.

'Don't worry, we'll get you there,' Paddy told me and, indeed, I was given England versus Georgia, and France against Italy in the new Autumn Nations Cup tournament introduced that November which would take me to that figure.

Paddy asked how I wanted to finish. I explained I was still planning to referee until the end of the 2020–21 season anyway, which had been severely disrupted by Covid-19, so it would be nice to round it all off where I'd started in the Six Nations back in 2007 – England versus Italy at Twickenham again, this time in the 2021 tournament. There just seemed to be a nice symmetry to that, but the reason more than anything was that my dad, other family members, Barrie and his family, could come and watch my last game, knowing that this was to be the final time on this stage. That would have been something very special, fully 14 years on from that first England versus Italy Six Nations game when my dad came to watch me referee at Twickenham and my mum, very ill at home with terminal cancer at the time, was wishing me the very best.

Paddy agreed, saying it was a good way to finish and told me to leave it with him for now. He spoke to his fellow selectors, rang back again and said that he thought that would be fine. So once the Six Nations appointments were made public, I could announce that England versus Italy would be my 101st and final match on the international stage. I would then hang up my Test whistle, whilst carrying on at the domestic level.

The exit strategy for me had been arranged. Or so I thought. I duly refereed my 100th match, France beating Italy in Paris on 28 November 2020, in the knowledge in my own mind that I would have one more game still to come.

By this stage it was announced that early in the new year Joël Jutge would return, yet again, as World Rugby referees' manager. As you've gathered by now, I've a huge amount of regard for him. He contacted me to explain he needed to find 12 quality referees for the next World Cup and, after the issues during the 2019 group games when World Rugby had gone public in saying the standard simply wasn't good enough, and the need to turn to the old stagers for the knockout matches, he was a little worried. Joël felt there was a lot of work to do and that work needed to start with immediate effect.

'At the moment I'm in trouble looking for those numbers,' Joël pointed out.

I fully respected Joël's honesty and reasoning, totally

understood where he was coming from, but explained the previous conversation I'd had with Paddy O'Brien; how I deliberately hadn't announced my retirement ahead of the Paris match on the understanding I was getting one more Test match. Joël asked for a few days to think about it, but clearly conversations were taking place behind the scenes because shortly afterwards Paddy, still heavily involved in the decision-making process, phoned to say they'd had a selection meeting and now weren't going to appoint me to the Six Nations after all.

If truth be told, I wasn't too hung up whether I finished in my 100th game, or 101st. What I was a little frustrated about was that having been under the impression I would get a Six Nations fixture, and told my dad, Barrie and others close to me to prepare for that one as my international swansong, I now had to hurriedly change my plans.

Things suddenly happened very quickly. I needed to speak to the WRU to arrange an announcement saying that I was retiring with immediate effect. We couldn't wait until after the Six Nations appointments were made public – which was due to happen in a matter of days – otherwise it might have come out in the headlines as 'Nigel Owens dropped from Six Nations'.

I didn't want that. Also, and I'm not intending to sound big-headed here, I didn't want a situation where there could be a bit of a backlash towards tournament organisers, from the media, pundits and the rugby public, demanding to know why Nigel Owens was not involved.

Derek Bevan, my old coach, was aware of what was going on, the very short timeframe we were left to work in and, as per usual, he provided me with some sound words of advice. 'Nige, if you don't announce your retirement now, I guarantee there will be a petition to get you another game, the public insisting you get a chance to go out properly.'

He argued that I had that kind of popularity and rugby fans would demand it was only right that I was given a fitting way in which to bow out, rather than the assumption that I'd been deemed not good enough to referee the Six Nations.

As always, Bev was talking sense. I didn't want that kind of fallout, or controversy, to be played out in the public domain. I didn't want any sense of bad feeling towards World Rugby or Six Nations organisers who, as I keep saying, by and large have been fantastic in their support down the years. I wanted a respectful ending and the only way to do that was to announce I was retiring at once.

Hey, leaving after my 100th cap wasn't exactly a bad way to go, was it? I was still bowing out on my own terms, to a degree, at the top. The only thing that disappointed me a bit was I thought we had agreed my exit timeline, yet that changed. I'm not saying that the game owes me anything, let me stress, because it most certainly doesn't. But when you've been around as long as I have, achieved so much, spent time away on international duty more than any other referee over almost a 20-year period, even agreed to drop everything to referee Australia and New Zealand for two weeks because Jérôme Garcès had fallen unwell, it might have been nice to stick to what I believed had been verbally agreed.

That's how the end came about. I didn't know it at the time, but Stade de France, Les Bleus against Italy, was to prove to be my final international appearance. As my 100th cap it was obviously a very special occasion anyway, but my emotions were rather strange going into it. Because of

Covid-19 there were no spectators. My family couldn't come out to watch. We were unable to head to the Champs-Elysées to celebrate afterwards because Paris was in lockdown.

If I'd known this would be the final time I would walk off an international field, I suspect I would have felt differently, perhaps been a little more emotional. But I was of the belief that my retirement would come a few months down the line. I wasn't to get the opportunity to know what that would really have felt like.

As I say, I don't referee for numbers, but of course I was proud to become the first to hit the 100 Tests landmark. There were some nice presents beforehand when France and Italy each gave me one of their jerseys. World Rugby presented me with a gold whistle and also put out a 'Congratulations Nigel' video on their social media platforms, where greats of the game paid me some lovely tributes.

My Scottish touch judge Mike Adamson and his colleague Sam Grove-White, the TMO, presented me with a bottle of whisky that had my name and the 100-Test achievement engraved on the glass. I received hundreds and hundreds of well done messages, including a particularly personal one from Rassie Erasmus, South Africa's 2019 World Cup winning coach, which I found touching. But every one of the messages meant a lot to me. There were so many of them that I'm still replying to a few today!

The game itself passed off uneventfully. A resurgent France won 36–5 to cement a place in the Autumn Nations Cup final against England the following week. But there was another special moment when the two sets of players lined up to form a guard of honour and clap and cheer me. Very humbling. Another example of the respect our great game shows.

They still didn't get any favouritism from me, mind!

France had an agreement with their Top 14 league that the leading players would not appear too often that autumn. As such, they had a second, almost even a third string out for this particular match, with Toulon scrum-half Baptiste Serin handed the honour of captaining his country for the first time.

I've always enjoyed his company on the field. He plays the game fairly and is respectful. Serin came into the changing room afterwards, French training top in hand, to present it to me as another memento of the occasion. 'It's been a privilege and a pleasure to have been refereed by you over the years – many congratulations,' Serin said. 'I want to give you my jersey really, but this is the first and probably only time I will be captain of France, so I'd like to keep it, if you don't mind.'

I totally understood, smiled and thanked him for the thought and gesture. Serin asked if he could have one of my referee jerseys in return – that reminds me, I must send one to him! Matthieu Jailbert, the French outside-half, had also said to me at the kick-off, 'You refereed my first cap and now I have the honour of being here for your 100th.' What lovely words, I thought.

I flew home from Paris still thinking I had one more Test match left, but in fact circumstances dictated that I ended up announcing my retirement just 13 days later. It wasn't quite the way I wanted it to end, but I still feel I went out on my own terms inasmuch as I was at the top of my game, getting matches on merit rather than out of any sympathy.

Derek Bevan, my former coach, and Ed Morrison, the ex-English referee, had always advised that, if I was still refereeing well, I should carry on as long as possible. But much better to leave the stage with people saying 'We're going to miss you' as opposed to 'About time you went, you're past your best.' This is often a hard balancing act and I notice some players across all sports get it wrong, and finish too late and find themselves criticised because their lofty standards have dropped. I certainly didn't want to be hanging on like that for the sake of it.

I guess three things helped make what was a very difficult call for me a little easier.

The first was World Rugby's stance towards me after the 2019 World Cup; the second was the farm and the amount of my time that was clearly going to start taking up; the third, believe it or not, was the Covid-19 situation.

Why that one? Because all of us being forced to stay at home actually made me want to do that even more, rather than head off on my rugby travels any longer. I had spent 20 years flying around the world, staying away for large chunks of time. While that sounds glamorous – and I'm certainly not complaining because rugby has always been wonderful to me and I stayed at fabulous hotels – I started to realise what I'd been missing. Even though these were strange times, and no-one really wanted lockdown, I also knew this is what I wanted most – to be around Barrie, my family and friends, those whose company I enjoy and love the most back home.

That said, whilst I hung up my Test whistle, I was more than prepared to carry on refereeing for at least another season in the United Rugby Championship, and help guide and bring through the next generation of referees as part of that, too. However, I could sense the end was coming. I didn't want to just hang about and be given the games no-one else really wanted. Thus I explained I was ready to go now and, after discussing this with Paul Adams, my referees' manager at the WRU, we thought a Welsh derby match might be a nice way to finish. There were a few of them coming up towards the end of the 2020–21 season.

My great mentor Derek Bevan had hung up his own whistle that way, a game between Cardiff and Llanelli at the Arms Park. It would have been good to follow in Bev's shoes. Funnily enough, I was running touch for him that day. Now Bev's house had been broken into a few months earlier. Lots of irreplaceable rugby memorabilia had been stolen, and in the clubhouse afterwards the legendary Cardiff chairman Peter Thomas stood up to make a speech.

'Derek, we're really grateful you're finishing your great career here at the Arms Park. You've always been welcome here with us. We love having you as referee.'

To which Bev muttered, 'You lying so-and-so. You've hated having me!'

Peter continued, 'We know your house was burgled and a lot of priceless items were taken, so to help you replace some of the material that simply can't be replaced, here's a framed Cardiff Blues jersey, signed by the players, as a token of our thanks.'

Bev walked up to the front, thanked Peter for the kind gesture, but said, 'There really was no need. I've already got one of these – it's the only f*****g thing the thieves didn't steal!'

Well, everyone just rolled around with laughter. Typical Bev. What a way to go out, his friends and family all enjoying the moment – and a few drinks – with him.

Sadly, because of Covid-19, the absence of fans and the abrupt ending, I didn't have that same opportunity. My last professional match came towards the end of March that season, like Bev at the Arms Park, as Cardiff Blues beat Edinburgh, 34–15. Again, like Bev, there was a bit of banter at the end when I walked past the Cardiff coach Dai Young, who was doing an after-match broadcast interview, and I flashed a quick V-sign. He burst out laughing, the interview had to be put on hold, everyone else turned round to see what the joke was, but Dai and I just had a quiet little smile between us, and didn't let on.

I had absolutely no idea at the time that that would be my final game. My contract still had more than a year to run, but no further opportunities were to arise. As with how my Test career finished, because of circumstances I wasn't able to go into a match knowing it would be the last one, enabling Barrie and my family, especially my dad, to come along and celebrate the occasion with me. Paul Adams pleaded my case, told Greg Garner, head of referees in our league at the time, that I'd made an awful lot of sacrifices over two decades, had even given up my Christmas once to do a Leinster versus Munster Boxing Day game in Ireland because they were struggling to get a neutral referee of suitable quality for such a big match.

It wasn't to be, though. I've heard people say that when your time is up you're just a number and certainly when you finish you move on. That's just the way it is, even as a World Cup final referee. I get that. My time just came a teeny bit earlier than I'd wanted it to, I guess.

So what next for me? Well my refereeing contract with the WRU officially ended in the summer of 2022, but I've got a new role with them now helping to coach younger referees – three of them for the time being – and also going to games to try to spot others with potential. Just as the likes of Bev and David McHugh mentored me, I'm now taking on that role myself, under the guidance of Paul Adams, with the new generation, passing on my own experience and knowledge in much the same way others helped me when I was at that age and looking to break through.

I have now also joined the United Rugby Championship as a selector, not just from the appointments side of things, but also viewing and assessing the performances of match officials. The main aim is to help them be the best they can be, and to try to make sure we continue to have some of the finest referees in the world in our league. It's a role I'm delighted to have taken on, an opportunity to put something back into this great game of ours which gave me so many opportunities of my own.

The highly-rated South African official Tappe Henning has taken over as the league's referees' manager and I'm really pleased to have the chance to work so closely with him. The league gets a lot of criticism, much of it very unfair in my eyes. There are a lot of good referees involved and I feel we are seeing improved performances across the board.

I'm still prepared to referee semi-pro and community matches, and I also do work with the Wales national squad, going into their training base at the Vale of Glamorgan sports complex, on the outskirts of Cardiff, to advise on law changes, what referees are cracking down on, what the players can, and more importantly, can't get away with.

I was often asked to do this when Warren Gatland was in charge and his successor, Wayne Pivac, also invited me into camp ahead of the 2021 Six Nations to give guidance on various issues, including discipline. I noticed Wales' first two opponents, Ireland and Scotland, each had players sent off, Peter O'Mahony and Zander Fagerson respectively, with Pivac's side winning against 14 men on each occasion. In Wales' third game, for the Triple Crown, England's indiscipline in giving away countless penalties saw them lose 40–24 at the Principality Stadium – so I'm glad the Welsh players clearly listened to what I had to say as they went on to lift the title!

I'm throwing myself into work on the farm. I've helped out on TV punditry from games. I'll do after-dinner speaking and I'm still prepared to referee a mix of Welsh Premiership games, the lower Welsh leagues, school games and Sunday morning rugby as and when I'm able to. With the semi-pro matches in the Welsh Premier I'd hoped to have some of the younger referees as my touch judges; then roles could be reversed and I'd run the line for them, aiding their development and helping to bring them up to the next level.

That advisory role for the Welsh team aside, the 2021 Six Nations was the first one I wasn't involved in for 14 years. But whilst it would have been nice to have had my England versus Italy swansong, I can honestly say I didn't miss being out there in the middle. Maybe it was because of the lack of crowds due to Covid-19, I'm not sure. The home and away support has historically helped to make this truly epic rugby competition the very best annual sporting event on the planet, as far as I'm concerned.

Fans or no fans, the intensity from the players certainly didn't let up, but clearly the atmosphere was never going to be the same. Actually, instead of refereeing I found myself up in the TV gantry doing commentary on Wales' matches for Welsh-language broadcaster S4C and also network TV. As I say, I can see myself doing more of this over the years, hoping to explain to the viewer, and indeed some of the pundits and commentators, why a referee has reached a particular decision and the process in law he considered to get to that point.

Referees receive an awful lot of criticism, don't I know it? I'm certainly not going to go on TV to defend the indefensible. If a clear error has been made, then I will say so. When the Frenchman Pascal Gaüzère refereed Wales versus England in Cardiff during the 2021 tournament, I feel he made two mistakes which led to Welsh tries. The first was in letting Dan Biggar take a quick crossfield penalty kick which enabled Josh Adams to score unopposed whilst the England players were gathered in a huddle by the posts. The reason they were there was because Pascal himself had asked the captain Owen Farrell to speak to his team about giving away too many penalties. In those circumstances, I feel he should have given Farrell more time to get the message across and also allowed England to re-set properly.

The second error, I believe, came when Louis Rees-Zammit knocked-on, lost control of the ball, in the build-up to try number two scored by Liam Williams. Those decisions were a little baffling to many and unfortunately I couldn't sugar-coat them. Nor will I defend other decisions that are clearly and obviously wrong. We are human after all. Referees can't get every single one correct. Myself included.

However, and this is hugely important, by the same token if a referee is being pilloried by pundits and public for something when I know he was correct in law, and that does happen all the time, I will explain why he was right and hopefully give viewers a clearer understanding of what was going through his mind. Those moments, in fact, will represent the vast majority of decisions, even if it is the odd controversy, like Gaüzère's from Wales versus England, which will tend to grab the headlines.

Thus I will strongly defend the referee when he is right and the world thinks he is wrong. Like the situation with French official Mathieu Raynal, who was heavily criticised at the end of the Australia versus New Zealand Bledisloe Cup game in September 2022 when he correctly sanctioned Wallaby Number 10 Bernard Foley for time-wasting. Instead of Foley clearing from a penalty, getting Australia up-field and winning the game, Raynal awarded the All Blacks a scrum and they scored a match-winning try of their own. Raynal had warned Foley previously to get on with it and this time, feeling those instructions had been ignored, he acted. Could he have dealt with it in a different way? Possibly, but he certainly wasn't wrong in law and, instead of referees being blamed, players need to take responsibility for what happens – especially in a case like this one, when Foley's fellow Wallabies had been screaming at him to get on with it.

I enjoy doing this punditry work. It's kept me involved at matches, including Six Nations ones, when I didn't know for certain whether I would have itchy feet at not being out there for a great old tournament which had become a fundamental part of me since 2007. I guess my emotions at not missing the refereeing tell me my decision to retire was the correct one. If I'd been missing it, clearly I'd have made an error.

Actually, it was during the first fallow week of the 2021 Six Nations when something happened which further made me realise it was the right time to go. I was refereeing Ospreys versus Zebre Parma in the PRO14 at the Liberty Stadium in

Swansea, not too far from my home, a rather low-key affair won 10–0 by the home side. Nothing particularly overly-exciting or dramatic about the 80 minutes of rugby, if I'm perfectly honest. It was OK, no worse, no better. And that's probably being kind!

What I will remember more was warming up before kick-off, the Ospreys in one part of the pitch, Zebre in the other half, when two of the Italian players approached me to say they were really glad to have me as referee that day – and asked if I minded having a photograph taken with them afterwards!

I didn't really know what to make of that, although this had also actually happened a few times over my last couple of seasons, in Toulouse, Japan and indeed out in Italy. That night at the Liberty Stadium I duly obliged. We got together in the tunnel area at the Liberty and the selfies were taken on the iPhones. The Italian duo were great about it, very polite, all smiles, clearly happy I'd posed with them. But isn't it the players who are supposed to be the famous sporting stars, the ones people ask for selfies or autographs?

Once it gets to the stage where players are requesting a photograph with the referee, then it's probably time to finish.

CHAPTER 11

Barrie and me, farming and the future

I FIRST MET my partner Baz, Barrie Jones-Davies to give him his full name, through mutual friends in Swansea back in July 2011, shortly before I headed out to New Zealand for the World Cup that year. We'd just got together, then suddenly I was off to the other side of the world for seven weeks.

That was perhaps indicative of something a lot of people don't always recognise; namely that being a full-time referee means you are away an awful lot, particularly when you reach the top level. You are tied up every weekend, and if there aren't any tournaments or matches, there are still refereeing camps. There's an awful lot of commitment and sacrifice and naturally that can make it very difficult for relationships at times, although Barrie has always been fully understanding of the demands that go with my profession.

Anyhow, we were introduced that evening in Swansea and arranged a first date shortly afterwards. The rendezvous point was to be the McDonald's car park in the west Wales town of Cross Hands, 15 miles north-west of Swansea and reasonably close to where we both lived. The plan was for us to drive there in separate cars, meet up, and then we'd head off in mine to a nearby restaurant. No, we didn't have a Big Mac and fries. It was a little more sophisticated than that!

At this point Barrie didn't know what I did for a living. The morning after the initial introduction he'd texted, 'Really good to meet you last night.' Then he asked what my job was.

I had to be a little coy, so I just replied, 'I work in sport.'

'What exactly?'

'I'll tell you when we meet.'

I didn't want a repeat of a previous blind date in Cardiff which didn't work out, but which ended in hilarious fashion. The person I met that night went home and told his friends, 'You'll never guess who I've been on a blind date with. Jonathan Davies.' I was absolutely creased up with laughter when I heard this back from a mutual friend. I couldn't wait to tell Jiffy. As well as being a great Welsh fly-half and also a rugby league legend-turned-expert TV commentator, he is also a great friend of mine.

I know Baz found my coyness a little frustrating at first, and probably wondered why I was being so vague. What was the reason for the secrecy? What's wrong with this guy, he must have thought! Barry subsequently said he wasn't sure whether I didn't want to spoil the surprise, or I was worried about putting him off!

Anyway, I parked up first at McDonald's. He arrived shortly afterwards to jump in with Nigel, whoever Nigel was, and by one of those sheer coincidences he pulled up in the car park spot right next to me. We hadn't seen one another at this point, so Barrie phoned to say, 'I'm here.' Suddenly, he could hear both our voices on the Bluetooth as I answered, looked over and saw it was me. The registration number, N1GE REF, then kind of gave the game away, I guess.

We hit it off straight away, were together for three and a half years, before breaking up. We were just at different points in our lives at the time, I guess. Barrie was starting university, en route to becoming a primary school teacher, and his mother wasn't well. That took up a lot of his time. I was obviously away an awful lot refereeing, so we amicably just chose to leave it.

However, we got back together in 2018 and pretty much picked up where we'd left off, not needing to go through the dating process of having to get to know one another. Barrie had a full-time job in a local school by that point. He'd bought a house and we just felt the time was right.

Thus, a relatively brief break-up aside, we've known each other for more than ten years. Our families are very close, his dad and mine get on well. We each come from a farming background, albeit Barrie perhaps isn't quite as passionate about it as I am. We live together in a lovely place in the village of Pontyberem, a few miles north of Llanelli and the M4, near to where I was brought up, although we're having a house built on a farm just up the road and will look to move in there hopefully in the summer of 2023.

I do enjoy Barrie's company and, as I've already stated in a previous chapter, his presence during the final two weeks of the 2019 World Cup out in Japan certainly helped me enjoy my refereeing more during the knockout stages. He had a week off for half-term and took another one as unpaid leave so that we could be together and I certainly needed, and greatly valued, his support. His school was also very supportive in allowing this once-in-a-lifetime opportunity, too.

Mind, poor Barrie must have wondered what he'd let himself in for when he first landed in the Far East. He isn't accustomed to travelling on his own, he's more used to going with friends, or in groups, so the plan was for me to meet him at the airport in Tokyo and take him in a car to where the hotel was. Trouble was, at the last minute an urgent referees' meeting was called because of the incident when South African official Jaco Peyper was photographed with Welsh fans mimicking the elbow motion which saw him red-card a France player in the quarter-final shootout between the two teams.

We were all summoned to be told there must be no repeat of that sort of thing. I knew that the time of the meeting clashed with when Barrie was due to land, but had no option but to go along. So I urgently left a message on his phone saying, 'Sorry, can't meet up at airport. Have heard the buses are fairly simple.'

I don't think he was best pleased to receive this when turning his phone on during one of the stopovers on a 17-hour flight. He also knew full well I'd never tried the buses, either!

Anyway, Barrie decided to get a taxi, blow the cost, and him being by my side certainly helped me relax when part of me was already counting down the days to going home. It's probably one of the reasons why I was able to referee that epic semi-final between England and New Zealand in Yokohama so well, putting me in with a shout of doing the final once more.

Barrie supports me. I also try to help him whenever he might have had a bad day at school, albeit it's not always easy to do so as I've never worked in that kind of environment as a teacher, although I did work at Maes-yr-yrfa school as a technician before taking up my role as a professional rugby referee with the Welsh Rugby Union back in December 2001. Our characters complement one another. I think Barrie will tell you himself that he's never seen me stressed when it comes to rugby, but he certainly has over farming issues, particularly when it comes to delivering calves, which we do ourselves, or cattle tests for TB. I'm the sort of person who wants to ring the vet all the time when it comes to our animals giving birth, something that invariably tends to happen at one, two or three in the morning, adding to the stress levels. Barrie calms me down, tends to see things more for what they are and doesn't panic so much.

He's also come to accept and understand when people come up and ask for a selfie, autograph, or want to talk rugby. At first Barrie felt like he was having to share me with the rest of the world. We'd be together in a restaurant, the cinema, or on a walk, and someone, somewhere, would come to interrupt. That wasn't always easy for Baz because our time together was precious. He knew there'd be another tournament coming up for me to referee at for weeks on end, or I'd be away doing a game over the weekend. Then he had to be teaching in school himself when I was perhaps free, so we needed to make the most of being together when we could. However, he knows this all comes with the territory and feels it's nice people want to chat with me, or ask for a photo, or an autograph.

Barrie is not massive on rugby. He'll watch Wales' matches, but tends more to dip in and out to check on the score rather than be glued to the TV. That said, he has always been very supportive of me in my games, and will try to watch those to see how I'm getting on. His dad is a big rugby fan, follows Llandovery RFC, while his twin brother Huw played rugby at youth level, although he now plays football to a decent standard. So we do talk about rugby every so often as families.

The next step for Barrie and myself, we hope, is to have children and we're going through the adoption process. We did look at surrogacy as an option, but I watched a couple of TV programmes and saw another couple who'd been through this, spent around £20,000, and it didn't work out in the end. The embryo didn't survive, so they ended up spending a lot of money for nothing. I'm certainly not against the sum involved, but my concern would be spending that money and it not working, going through the process again, same result. That rollercoaster of emotions, more than the loss of the money, would have been too much for either of us.

So we decided adoption would be a good way of giving a child a really good start in life, while obviously having a sibling, or two, of our own. I love kids, have always had my little cousins around and thoroughly enjoyed playing with them, reading to them, watching videos together. We feel it would be wonderful to bring up a child, help develop his or her personality, teach them the kind of good manners I myself had drilled into me by my own mum and dad back in the day.

The adoption process is quite intense really, and indeed an eye-opener. The initial introductions came in September 2021. We then started an adoption course three months later. That involved meeting a social worker every Friday from 10am to 3pm – Barrie obviously having to take time off school, who again were hugely supportive – where we'd talk, listen to guest speakers, mainly people who'd been adopted giving their own experiences. The authorities have wanted to know everything about us, our backgrounds, our views on certain issues, our financial situation, what happened in our own childhood. No stone was left unturned, which I guess I can understand.

The person leading the course would explain the type of children who come up for adoption, where the kids have sometimes come from, their background, which can often be the worst-case scenario of being neglected or abused. It's quite heartbreaking when you sit there listening to it all, but things appear to be different to 40 years ago when a lot of children were given up at birth and nobody would tell you you'd been adopted.

These days, when children are taken away for their own good, often with some sort of trauma, you're encouraged to tell them from an early stage that they've been adopted and indeed the reasons why. There's also a letterbox system where you're encouraged to write a letter to the birth parents to let them know how the child is getting on, and they can respond if they wish to.

We're looking to move into our new house by the spring or summer of 2023. Having one or two children there with us would be fantastic, probably aged up to four, possibly brothers or sisters – something social services are keen upon as they wish to keep families together where possible. The feeling is it would be better for the child, or children, to be settled in our new home, rather than come to our current house and have to move again a few months down the line, with the potential stress that that could cause them.

There one or two things that concern me a little. If someone in the local area gives up a child, and someone else says, 'Oh, Nigel Owens has recently adopted', it would be easy to put two and two together. For that reason, we'd probably look to adopt from further afield. The adoption agency at Carmarthenshire County Council would be looking for a match outside of the county for us anyway, but still the concern is there.

I suppose the other thing that worries me is that a child is taken away for a reason, and you try to bring him or her up in your own personality. Then at the age of ten or later, the birth parents might come along to try to drag him or her back. Possibly to a bad way again, too. I guess all you can do is trust that you have brought up that child in the right way, given a truly loving home, and hope that it does not happen.

However, despite the concerns, the good would clearly outweigh the bad as far as Barrie and I are concerned.

The house we're having built is on Brynwicket Farm, not too far from our current address in Pontyberem. The land used to belong to an old couple, and their doctor son, who lives away from the area, said that he was delighted to learn of my interest in purchasing it. His mum and dad were big fans of mine, he explained, and they would have wanted the farm to stay in local hands.

It means we now have close on 90 acres of farmland in total and are also renting a further 48 acres. My new life, after refereeing, is as a farmer. We look after 75 pedigree Herefords. We may also have a couple of chickens when the new property is ready – I do like having some fresh eggs for breakfast, I must say – and always love having dogs around.

Farming and refereeing, of course, are two entirely different professions, albeit quite similar in a way (you're always outdoors for starters). So how did it come to this, you might well wonder? Well, my first dream, at the age of eight, was always to be a farmer, not a rugby referee. This was as a result of my upbringing. My dad was one of seven, my mum one of six, and they both came from farming families. My grandparents owned a smallholding and kept chickens and horses. This is where we lived until I was the age of five. My mum's aunt Gloria and her husband Graham also owned one, and farmed Pentwyn Farm, Llannon, where I'd be during the school holidays helping out with their son Andrew. So it's always been in the blood for me, while Barrie's family, too, have a farming background.

When I left school I initially worked on a farm, but gradually the demands of refereeing took over. However, I always retained my dream of owning my own farm one day. It can be difficult to get into, unless you marry a farmer's daughter – and that was never going to happen, was it!

That said, whilst refereeing I started to keep an eye out for a smallholding that might come up in the area. I didn't wish to move away from friends and family, and I managed to persuade Noel Richards, a neighbouring farmer at Coedmoelion, to sell me the three fields around my house, which came to 13 acres. A further 15 acres quickly became available up the road, so I bought those as well.

This was a dream come true really – 28 acres, ten cattle to start with. A friend then told me the old couple's place was coming up for sale and asked if I'd be interested in buying a bit more land. That was a further 60 acres. The farmhouse needed to be gutted and rebuilt, which it will be into our new home. So bit by bit we increased the herd from ten to 15 to 75 pedigree Herefords.

We have a farmhand helper called Rhys Jones, who farms nearby in Llannon, but myself and Barrie do most of the work ourselves. Well, I do! That means mucking out, feeding, strawing, mowing hay, moving the cattle from one field to another for fresh grass, dosing them with fly spray. Everything you can think of, really. It's physical work, albeit mostly done by machinery, but I enjoy it. It's certainly different to being a professional referee, let me tell you that.

As I say, Barrie and myself have even delivered calves ourselves in the middle of the night – a darned sight more stressful and pressurised experience than me doing the World Cup final, I promise you. If a calf is coming out backwards you have to pull it, or else it will die. Believe me, these are real pressures when they are happening right in front of you. We've been very lucky to have great vets at ProStock, husband and wife Rhys and Sarah-Jane, who are always ready to help and advise and who have become great friends of ours now. Indeed, the farming community is a close-knit one and people are always ready to assist, just like Nev Roberts from Wern Farm in Drefach where I used to work after leaving school.

My dad and Barrie's dad will also come over during the week to help out, mend some fencing, cut a tree that has fallen, anything that needs doing. They love it, too, keeping it in the family.

So why did I choose the Hereford breed? Well they're very docile animals, lovely to look at and easy to look after. They also produce premium, highly sought-after meat. Not that we're necessarily supplying the meat market, we're more into selling and breeding. It started with a few pedigree heifers after I was introduced to a guy called Robin Quinn who was looking to sell, and it has just grown from there.

When you're a registered breeder you're obliged to have a name for the herd. A good friend of mine, Neil Bartholemew, suggested I name it after my late mum, whose name was Rachel Mairwen, but was known to everybody as Mair. So ours are called Pedigree Mairwen Hereford. The quality of bloodline is important and every calf that's born here on our farm starts off with the name Mairwen.

While farming invariably takes up a lot of my time, I'm obviously still very active in other areas. I have my new contract with the Welsh Rugby Union to help coach younger referees. I'll watch their games at the weekend, conduct reviews of their performances during the week to advise, encourage and suggest areas where they've done well and how they can improve further. I'd like to thank Paul Adams for this opportunity and his support over the years, not just as my referees' manager, but also as a fellow referee for many years together, too. We shared some great times. I've also taken on another role as a selector on the United Rugby Championship Match Officials' panel, which I'm really excited about. Hopefully we can help bring through and guide the next generation in our league towards the very top of world refereeing.

I also do after-dinner speaking, as well as keynote talks at functions during the day, while there's TV, radio and newspaper work, too. So there's a great variety to what I do and that's been important in helping me with the transition of finishing as a referee. What I didn't want was a regular nine-to-five office job. I needed to retain flexibility during the week, as I had become accustomed to during my years at the top level, and I've got that in terms of being able to mix things up a bit.

Far from having withdrawal symptoms over hanging up the whistle, the next few years are going to be exciting for me and I'm really looking forward to life after refereeing. Clearly, however, what has happened during my career in rugby has defined me to a degree. It's been an incredible journey, particularly after the dark days I've tried to be candid about in this book, and I hope you've enjoyed coming on that journey with me.

Thank you for taking the time to read this autobiography. I hope it's brought a smile to your face, maybe even a tear or two to the eye at times, and that you've learned something. For those who, like me, have been through dark times, I hope my story can help you, prove that you can get through the trauma, however difficult it may seem at the time, and learn to live with it, be a better person by being honest, open and indeed your real self.

Please don't try to be perfect, nobody can be in life. I never refereed a perfect game of rugby – although I'd like to think I came close a couple of times! We don't live in a perfect world, so don't let the perfect be the enemy of the good. Being perfect is unachievable; what achievable is to be a good person who cares for those around you, looks out for them, and who is honest. With yourself and with others. Crikey, don't I know that.

From my story in this book you can see how being honest changed my own life for the good and I just want to say a massive thank you, right from the bottom of my heart, to everyone who has supported me on the way – family, friends, rugby powers-that-be, players, coaches, fellow referees, supporters everywhere across the world. To the countless people, men, women, boys, girls, who've come up to say hello at games, or in the street, asked for selfies, autographs, or who've just wanted to chat about rugby, indeed life in general, I hope I've helped you a little, just as so many have helped me.

Thank you everybody. Take care and enjoy.

Hwyl fawr (that's Welsh for so long, for those who don't know).

Diolch. Love to all.

Nigel's
100-Test career

2003

Game 1 (16 February): Portugal 34–30 Georgia (Lisbon)

2005

Game 2: Japan 12–44 Ireland (Osaka)

Game 3: Argentina 12–28 Samoa (Buenos Aires)

2006

Game 4: Argentina 26–0 Uruguay (Buenos Aires)

Game 5: Italy 18–25 Australia (Rome)

2007

Game 6: Portugal 16–15 Morocco (Lisbon)

Game 7: England 20–7 Italy (Twickenham)

Game 8: New Zealand 26–12 Australia (Auckland)

Game 9: Ireland 23–20 Italy (Belfast)

Game 10: Argentina 33–3 Georgia (Lyon)

Game 11: Scotland 42–0 Romania (Murrayfield)

Game 12: Australia 55–12 Fiji (Montpellier)

2008

Game 13: France 26–21 Ireland (Paris)

Game 14: Italy 23–20 Scotland (Rome)

Game 15: New Zealand 37–20 England (Auckland)

Game 16: France 42–17 Pacific Islanders (Montbéliard)

Game 17: England 6–42 South Africa (Twickenham)

2009

Game 18: Ireland 30–21 France (Dublin)

Game 19: Scotland 26–6 Italy (Murrayfield)
Game 20: South Africa 31–19 New Zealand (Durban)
Game 21: New Zealand 29–32 South Africa (Hamilton)
Game 22: England 16–9 Argentina (Twickenham)
Game 23: Ireland 15–10 South Africa (Dublin)

2010
Game 24: Scotland 9–18 France (Murrayfield)
Game 25: Australia 27–17 England (Perth)
Game 26: South Africa 22–29 New Zealand (Johannesburg)
Game 27: Ireland 21–23 South Africa (Dublin)

2011
Game 28: Scotland 18–21 Ireland (Murrayfield)
Game 29: Canada 34–18 Russia (Esher)
Game 30: Ireland 9–20 England (Dublin)
Game 31: Fiji 49–25 Namibia (Rotorua)
Game 32: New Zealand 83–7 Japan (Hamilton)
Game 33: Australia 67–5 USA (Wellington)
Game 34: South Africa 13–5 Samoa (North Shore City, Auckland)
Game 35: New Zealand 33–10 Argentina (Auckland)

2012
Game 36: France 30–12 Italy (Paris)
Game 37: England 30–9 Ireland (Twickenham)
Game 38: New Zealand 42–10 Ireland (Auckland)
Game 39: New Zealand 22–19 Ireland (Addington, Christchurch)
Game 40: New Zealand 22–0 Australia (Auckland)
Game 41: Australia 26–19 South Africa (Perth)
Game 42: France 33–6 Australia (Paris)
Game 43: England 15–16 South Africa (Twickenham)

2013
Game 44: Italy 23–18 France (Rome)
Game 45: France 23–16 Scotland (Paris)
Game 46: Argentina 26–51 England (Buenos Aires)
Game 47: New Zealand 24–9 France (New Plymouth)
Game 48: Australia 14–13 Argentina (Perth)
Game 49: South Africa 27–38 New Zealand (Johannesburg)
Game 50: Ireland 22–24 New Zealand (Dublin)

2014

Game 51: France 26–24 England (Paris)

Game 52: Ireland 46–7 Italy (Dublin)

Game 53: New Zealand 20–15 England (Auckland)

Game 54: Russia 23–15 Zimbabwe (Krasnoyarsk)

Game 55: South Africa 28–10 Australia (Cape Town)

Game 56: Argentina 21–17 Australia (Mendoza)

Game 57: England 21–24 New Zealand (Twickenham)

Game 58: France 29–26 Australia (Paris)

2015

Game 59: France 15–8 Scotland (Paris)

Game 60: England 55–35 France (Twickenham)

Game 61: Australia 24–20 South Africa (Brisbane)

Game 62: New Zealand 41–13 Australia (Auckland)

Game 63: England 21–13 Ireland (Twickenham)

Game 64: Tonga 10–17 Georgia (Gloucester)

Game 65: South Africa 34–16 Scotland (Newcastle)

Game 66: France 9–24 Ireland (Millennium Stadium)

Game 67: New Zealand 62–13 France (Millennium Stadium)

Game 68: New Zealand 34–17 Australia (Twickenham) World Cup final

2016

Game 69: Saint Vincent and the Grenadines 0–48 Jamaica (Kingstown)

Game 70: France 21–31 England (Paris)

Game 71: Fiji 23–18 Tonga (Suva)

Game 72: Australia 40–44 England (Sydney)

Game 73: Australia 23–17 South Africa (Brisbane)

Game 74: New Zealand 37–10 Australia (Auckland)

Game 75: Italy 10–68 New Zealand (Rome)

2017

Game 76: Ireland 19–9 France (Dublin)

Game 77: Argentina 34–38 England (San Juan)

Game 78: New Zealand 35–29 Australia (Dunedin)

Game 79: New Zealand 57–0 South Africa (North Shore City, Auckland)

Game 80: France 17–18 South Africa (Paris)

2018

Game 81: France 13–15 Ireland (Paris)

Game 82: Scotland 25–13 England (Murrayfield)

Game 83: Japan 28–0 Georgia (Toyota)

Game 84: New Zealand 34–36 South Africa (Wellington)

Game 85: Ireland 54–7 Italy (Chicago)

Game 86: France 26–29 South Africa (Paris)

2019

Game 87: England 44–8 France (Twickenham)

Game 88: USA 13–10 Samoa (Suva)

Game 89: Tonga 33–23 Canada (Lautoka, Fiji)

Game 90: France 32–3 Scotland (Nice)

Game 91: England 57–15 Ireland (Twickenham)

Game 92: Japan 30–10 Russia (Tokyo)

Game 93: Italy 48–7 Canada (Fukuoka)

Game 94: England 39–10 Argentina (Tokyo)

Game 95: USA 19–31 Tonga (Osaka)

Game 96: New Zealand 46–14 Ireland (Tokyo)

Game 97: England 19–7 New Zealand (Yokohama)

2020

Game 98: France 24–17 England (Paris)

Game 99: England 40–0 Georgia (Twickenham)

Game 100 (28 November): France 36–5 Italy (Paris)

OTHER INTERNATIONALS

Southern Kings v British and Irish Lions

Wales v Barbarians

England v Barbarians

Scotland v Barbarians

New Zealand v Barbarians

STATISTICS

Tests as referee: 100

Tests as assistant referee: 101

Tests as TMO: 9

Total: 210

FOUR WORLD CUPS

Rugby World Cup matches as referee: 19

Record-holder for most Six Nations matches as referee: 21

World Rugby Referee Award recipient in 2015

Yellow cards: 58
Red cards: 3
First yellow card: Daisuke Ohata (Japan v Ireland, 12 June 2005)
First red card: Napolioni Nalaga (Pacific Islanders v France,
15 November 2008)

Tries scored in his Tests: 495
Points scored in his Tests: 4,591

TEAMS REFEREED
Number of teams refereed: 25
Portugal, Georgia, Japan, Ireland, Argentina, Samoa, Uruguay, Italy,
Australia, Morocco, England, New Zealand, Scotland, Romania, Fiji,
France, Pacific Islanders, South Africa, Russia, Canada, Namibia,
Zimbabwe, Tonga, Saint Vincent and the Grenadines and Jamaica

Team refereed the most: New Zealand, 25 Tests from 2007–19

Top five teams by Tests: New Zealand (25), England (24), France (24),
Ireland (20), Australia (19)

Only 13 Tests have not involved a Six Nations or Rugby Championship
team

7 HEINEKEN CUP FINALS
2008: Munster 16–13 Toulouse (Millennium Stadium)
2009: Leinster 19–16 Leicester (Murrayfield)
2012: Leinster 42–13 Ulster (Twickenham)
2015: Clermont 18–24 Toulon (Twickenham)
2016: Racing 9–21 Saracens (Lyon)
2017: Clermont 17–28 Saracens (Murrayfield)
2020 Exeter 31–27 Racing (Ashton Gate, Bristol)

3 CHALLENGE CUP FINALS

6 CELTIC LEAGUE/PRO12 FINALS

(FACTS AND FIGURES COURTESY OF WELSH RUGBY UNION)